TRADITIONAL POTTERS

From the Andes to Vietnam

Isabelle C. Druc

Deep University Press

TRADITIONAL POTTERS

From the Andes to Vietnam

Isabelle C. Druc

Deep University Press

Copyright © 2016 by Poiesis Creations Ltd - Deep University Press
Member of Independent Book Publishers Association (IBPA)

All rights reserved. No part of this book may be reproduced in any form or by any means without written permission from the publisher.

For permissions, contact: publisher@deepuniversity.net

ISBN 978-1-939755-24-7 (Paperback)
Library of Congress Cataloging-in-Publication Data

Keywords: 1. Ceramics. 2. Ethnography. 3. Traditional crafts. 4. Ceramic production. 5. Travel diary. 6. Druc, Isabelle C.
Target audience: general public, ceramists, students, professors and researchers in ceramics, ethnography, archaeology, arts and ceramic analysis.
Version 1

Front cover: Biển producing a small cooking pot on the wheel, Phạm Văn Tình's workshop, Phu Lang, Vietnam. Photo: I. Druc 2014.
Back cover: Cooking pots waiting to be packed and sent to the market. Workshop of the family of Manuel Heras Ocas, Mollepampa, Cajamarca, Peru. Photo: I. Druc, 2010.

TRADITIONAL POTTERS
From the Andes to Vietnam

CONTENTS

1	Introduction	7
2	Potters of the Andes	11
3	Potters of Argentina	47
4	Potters of Mexico	53
5	Potters of Turkey	63
6	Potters of Thailand	77
7	Potters of Vietnam	87
8	From the producer to the table	103
9	A pot under a microscope	117
10	Conclusion	123
Acknowledgements		125

Mingei: art of the people, after Sōetsu Yanagi, who considered that "the purest and most beautiful type of craft came from the untutored craftsman who worked guided only by tradition". Quoted from Andrew Maske, 2009, 165. See also Bernard Leach 1967.

1 Drying pots in the patio of the workshop of Phạm Văn Tình, Phu Lang, Vietnam.

2 Potters of the Andes

3 Modern jar with traditional patterns, Manya workshop, Cajamarca, Peru.

The Andes of Peru, Ecuador and Bolivia are home to many communities of potters, from the coastal valleys to the altiplano. The majority of the potters are found in mid to upper valleys, in the inter-Andean regions and high plateaus, generally in areas where water and clay resources are found. Due to the cold climate in the high elevation of the Cordillera, potters often work on a seasonal basis, during the dry months of the year, between May and October. For extracting clay, and for the pots to dry and be fired, sunny, non-rainy days are needed. The rest of the year, these potters work at other tasks, in their fields or in other towns.

Potting communities are also found in the lowlands and Amazonian regions east of the Cordillera but will not be presented here. Traditional potters in Chile and Argentina, further down the Andean Cordillera, are discussed in the next chapter. Having spent many years investigating in Peru, most of the potters and communities illustrated here are from that country, in particular from the highlands of two departments, Ancash and Cajamarca, where I conducted most of my fieldwork. They display an interesting range of ceramic practices and manufacturing techniques, characteristic of traditional Andean potters at large.

The wheel to shape pots is not used traditionally in the Andes and was only introduced in South America after the Spanish conquest. The same with glazing or varnishing, and with firing in a kiln, as a permanent, closed structure as we know it in Europe or Asia. Another constant for many Andean traditional productions is the use of temper, as a second or third material added to the clay base to make it suitable for manufacture, less plastic, and with more structure.

12 Potters of the Andes

4 Wikimedia map by AgainErik, Creative Commons. Modified by the author to show sites and regions mentioned in the text.

5 Village of Yacya in June, 3600 m high, in the Conchucos region of highland Ancash, Peru.

The main traditional production techniques found in the Andes are coiling, paddle-and-anvil, and different molding techniques, using bivalve molds as support or to shape part of the ware. These techniques were used already in Pre-Columbian times, as evidenced by tools or molds found in archaeological excavations or tombs, or by analyzing ancient fragments. Modeling was also used, particularly for figurines and certain multicomponent wares. Some techniques can also be combined, like starting with a coil or a flat disc upon which a coil is added, and then using a paddle-and-anvil to lift the walls or to decorate the ware. Several of these techniques can be observed in the Department of Ancash in the central Andes. These different potters and traditions are found on both side of the White Cordillera, the highest range of the Peruvian Andes, with peaks above 6600 m.

Example of the coiling technique is illustrated in the next pages, with Anaseta Ocaña Janampa, from the highland village of Yacya, in Conchucos on the eastern side of the White Cordillera. Anaseta builds jars out of a few thick coils. Each coil is pinched and lifted with the hands to form the wall of the jar (7-14). Between each coil addition, the pot needs to dry a little or else the wet clay will not hold the weight of the next coil. Yacya, Mallas and Acopallca are communities where women are the potters. Tools are kept at a minimum: a corncob, a stick, a cloth, a gourd fragment, and a small ceramic or wooden plate upon which the ware is made then dried (6). Each region has its variants.

6 Potter Felicitas Rojas Gregoria with her potting tools. Yacya, Ancash, Peru, 2004.

14 Potters of the Andes

7

Anaseta Ocaña Janampa de Inca Mori, Yacya, Ancash, Peru.

8

9

Potters of the Andes 15

10

11

12 Reproduced from Druc 2013 fig. 3, with permission from the Journal of Anthropological Research.

Production used to be more intense in the past. Now it only spreads over two-three weeks during the dry season.

16 Potters of the Andes

13

14

15 A potter's basket, where the woman stores her tools. She takes the basket with her if she has to produce outside her home. The raw materials and clay body will be prepared for her at the place of production.

16

17

When women are the potters, as is the case in this part of the Ancash Department, the men of the family are helping: husband, brother, brother in law, son. In Yacya, Mallas and Acopalca, they are in charge of getting the material to prepare the ceramic paste. In that region, slate temper is added to the clay. The slate is mined from sources four or five hours away by foot in the mountain above. Clay is acquired closer to the community. The materials are crushed, sieved, and mixed together with water, tramped by foot and kneaded by hand. Sr Inca Mori (above), from the village of Yacya, is the husband of Anaseta. He crushes the slate on a big flat stone in the back of the house. The men are also in charge of getting fuel to fire the wares.

When no family men are there - because they traveled to a town to work or are sick, or if the potter is a widow - the women must pay laborers to help. As it raises the cost of production, manufacture can be postponed or halted for some years. Also, the younger generation does not want to become potters. The work is too harsh on the body and revenues too low and insecure. Unfortunately, this is the case in many communities across South America.

18 Quarry where slate is extracted for use as temper to give more strength to the clay base. This mine is above 4000 m high, in the region east of Chacas, Ancash, Peru.

19 Crushing station in the fields below the mine.

Figures 13 and 19 are reproduced from Druc 2000, fig. 2. and 4, with permission from the Institut Français d'Etudes Andines.

20 *Achupalla* plant in the Andes. 21 Harvested and dried *achupalla*.

In this region, *Achupalla,* a type of bromeliacea is used as combustible for firing. In other places, wood, cow dung, straw or a combination of the above is used.

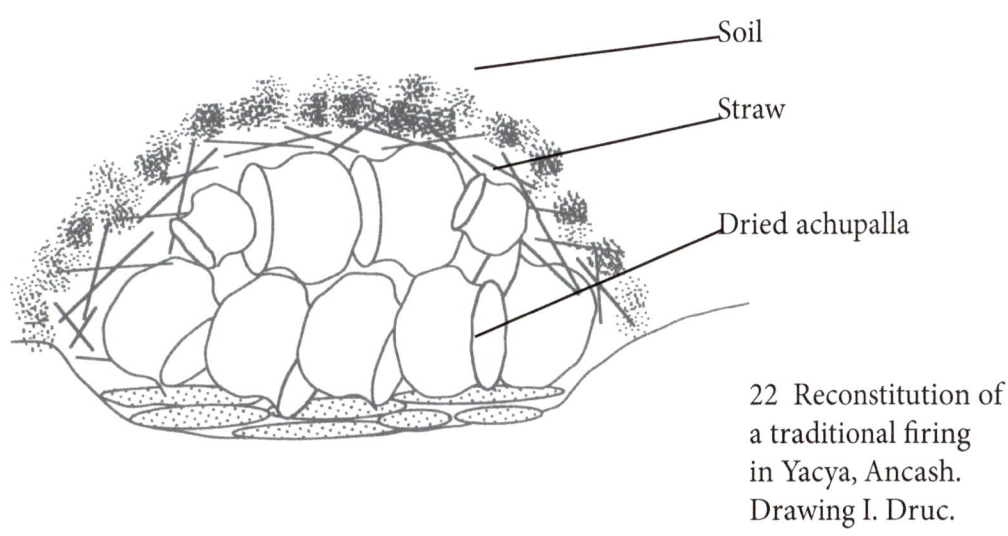

22 Reconstitution of a traditional firing in Yacya, Ancash. Drawing I. Druc.

In the region of Huari, the firing of the wares is done by a specialist called 'tambero' and his aids. A hollow pit is dug in a field, and the pots are laid on top of dried *achupalla*. The firing takes from a couple hours if the pots are simply covered with straw to an entire night if they are covered with dirt. The latter prevents oxygen access and the wares acquire a darker color.

23 Firing in Acopalca, Ancash. Photo Javier Salas. Used with permission.

24 Pulling out the still hot pots from the fire. Photo Javier Salas. Used with permission.

Potters of the Andes 21

Producing during the dry season takes advantage of the agricultural cycle and many celebrations around it. The pots can be exchanged for agricultural products that have just been harvested. Fairs and markets occur during that time and village festivals are an incentive to produce pots for exchange. Jars are also needed to prepare the fermented corn beer known as *chicha*, an important part of any social meeting and festivals.

25 The village of Acopalca, Ancash, getting ready for the annual celebration of the village patron.

26 Sra Fernandez Tello with bags of material for ceramic production. Acopalca, Ancash, Peru.

22 Potters of the Andes

Sra Maria Mercedez Vargas Hidalgo of Mallas and her husband Sr. Aureliano Trujillo Huerta stopped producing many years ago, for lack of demand. Sr. Aureliano used to prepare the ceramic paste and fire the pots. He says that people are not interested anymore to buy earthen ware pots. Difficulty of obtaining the material and no men around (but not in the case of Sra Vargas), are other reasons given to stop production. Alternatively, reasons to produce include additional income as was the case for Anaseta and her husband, who needed to help their son who was in charge of the village celebration that year.

Tarica in the Callejon de Huaylas

Due to change in society, products' demand, cooking habits, tastes, industrialization, rural exodus, and very low profit, pottery production of utilitarian wares has much decreased. Where entire villages used to produce for the surrounding region, now only a few families still work in the trade. Isolated potters are also found here and there, producing on demand.

There are exceptions, of course. Tarica, is a small village, at 3200 m in the Callejon de Huaylas, a high valley on the western side of the White Cordillera. It has been a production center in the past, benefitting from the warmer microclimate of the valley. This makes it a very hospitable place to live, with many towns, villages, and markets to distribute local products. In this valley, potting is a male activity. No woman should engage in ceramic production, as it is believed she will get sick from working the clay. Women can however help decorate the pots. The paddle-and-anvil technique is used, as it is the case in much of northern Peru. In Tarica, the paddle helps strengthening the walls, which are built out of coils upon a flat clay disc, as illustrated by the work of Nicanor Saavedra Rodriguez below (31-33). The 'anvil' in this area is a mushroom-shape clay tool (in Nicanor's right hand fig. 29).

29

31

30 Set of wooden paddles and ceramic plates upon which to form the pots.

24   Potters of the Andes

32

33

Nicanor in 2012 and his wife Sra Olimpia Norabueno León.

34

In the Callejon de Huaylas, production season can extend from March till November, longer than in other high regions of Peru. Some potters even extend the production throughout the year, albeit much less intensive, storing their pots till the weather allows firing them. In the past 25 years or so, the production has diversified and technology has changed. Decorative, modern and tourist wares are produced with a different clay, the kick wheel, and the pottery is fired in electric kilns. This shift can be traced back to the 70s when Tarica and other villages were greatly affected by a major landslide. Tarica's center was rebuilt and a foreign ceramist team funded a ceramic school, introducing the wheel, glazing and modern kilns in the region. Nicanor's son follows that trend. Traditionally, potting in Tarica was a male activity, now women participate more in the production of molded and modeled tourist wares.

35 Nicanor's daughter decorating jars with kaolin clay. These white lines are the hallmark of the traditional wares from Tarica.

Nicanor used to travel to villages higher up in the Cordillera to offer his service and produce on-site. His wife accompanied him and would cook for him while he was producing. They would leave for one or two weeks, bringing with them all the material they needed to produce pottery. They occupied a house on the outskirts of the village they visited, and people would come to them to place orders.

Nicanor acquires his clay and temper from quarries in the mountain, up to seven hours away by foot. He mixes two to four different clays, more or less plastic. The clay paste is kneaded by foot (36), and again by hand in smaller batches, the amount needed for the day production. The rest is kept damp under a plastic.

36

37-40 Nicanor fires his pots placing the wares on a bed of wood and straw, and covering them again with straw. Two rows of broken pots contain the kiln structure. The fire is tended for about two hours, after which the wares are usually done, but let to cool down during the night. Very early the next morning, they are packed in straw and brought to market. Firing during harvest time means availability of straw, which Nicanor's sons gathered from the field next to the house.

37

Potters of the Andes 27

38

39

40

The paddle-and-anvil technique seen in the Callejon de Huaylas is also shared by potters west and east of the Cordillera. However production has dwindled and only a few potters continue the trade. This is the case of Lucio Vega (40) from Ichicchinlla, a neighborhood of Chinlla, a highland village at 3410 m between the towns of Chacas and San Luis, in northern Conchucos, Ancash.

The plates on which he forms his pots (42-43) bear his mark, which will be imprinted on the bottom of the pots.

41

42

In 1997, no road allowed driving to the village. The 45 minute uphill trek from the dirt road below was done daily by teachers who lived in other towns or villages. There also was no electricity. By 2007, the situation had somewhat improved, but it was still easier to reach the village by foot, across fields, rather than wait for a theoretical minibus ride.

43

44

45

Lucio Vega is also a farmer (above in 2007), which allows him to put some food on the table when demand for pots are scarce or lacking. In the Chacas-San Luis region the men are the potters, unlike in Yacya and Acopalca 70 km further south. The two regions share the use of crushed slate, but not the technology nor the gender organization of labor. This difference between two neighboring regions is linked to the socio-cultural and political organization of the territories at the time of the Incas and early colonial period.

The use of crushed slate as temper can also be traced back many centuries. It was already used before the arrival of the Spanish and this tradition continues today. In the villages, potters adapted to the taste and needs of the new settlers and the Spanish church without changing the materials and manufacturing techniques they were accustomed to. In the cities, the story is different and big workshops were established, implementing European traditions and techniques.

Learning and adapting

46

47

Sr. Rosas Atanacio Murga (46-47) from Cunca used to produce earthenwares in the lower coastal Valley of Sechin, a valley descending from the Cordillera towards the Pacific Ocean. He learned the trade in the Callejon de Huaylas by observing how the potters were producing their wares. He was one of the few potters established in the valley, and mined nearby river terraces for clay and temper (46) to produce his pots.

48 As, Sr. Murga, Sr. Lindo from Calpoc, a hamlet 1200 m in the upper Casma valley, learned the trade in the Callejon de Huaylas, on the other side of the mountain range where he now lives. He had to adapt to local materials and made his own anvils, which are slightly different than the ones from the Callejon de Huaylas.

Potters of Mangallpa

Another production center where the paddle-and-anvil technique is used is Mangallpa, in the Department of Cajamarca in the northern Andes. In this village some 300 families are still engaged in the production of cooking pots and jars. Their wares are renown over a wide area, thanks to the habit of the Mangallpa potters to produce outside their village, sometimes up to several days walk away. They are itinerant potters, traveling with their tools and sieved material. They leave for several days or weeks during the dry season, on foot or with donkeys in the past, or by truck now. They adapt to the requisites of the villagers for whom they are producing, both in terms of forms and decoration.

In Mangallpa, production is carried out by the men. They do not use potter's plates and form the ware out of a lump of clay, which is shaped with a plain, wooden paddle, counter-balancing the hits with a round cobble stone. Coiling is not used. When still slightly wet or leather-hard, decoration is beaten down with another wooden paddle, this time with fine grooves, which imparts a distinctive pattern onto the surface of the wares. This is a way to recognize that the pots are from Mangallpa. Other designs or differences in the grooves or their spacing characterize other ceramic communities.

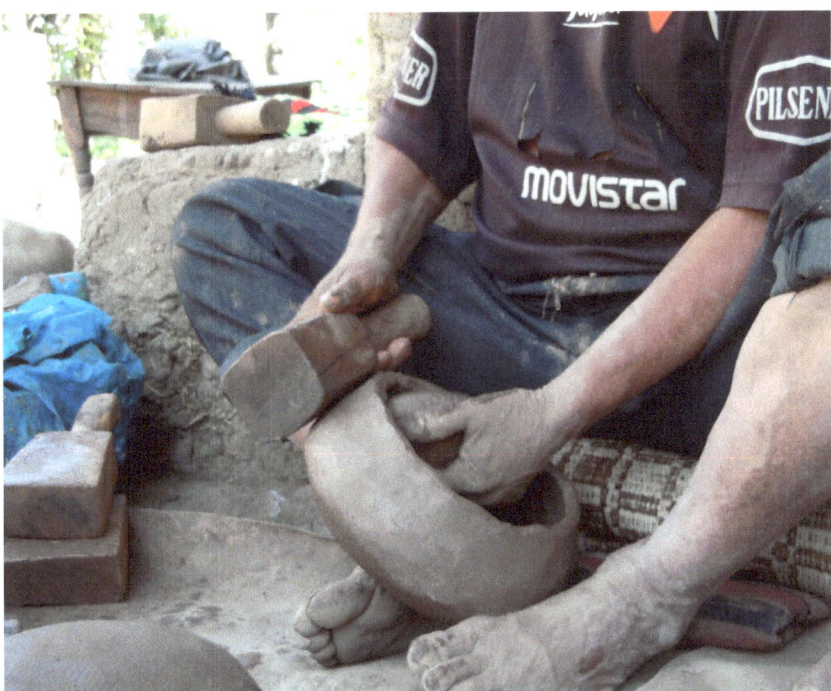

49 Production of Sr. Miguel Tanta Aguilar, Mangallpa, Cajamarca.

50 The village of Mangallpa, in the San Pablo district, Department of Cajamarca, Peru, at 2200 meters elevation.

Each Mangallpa potter can produce some 100 pots in a week. If we count that 200 potters are at work (not all are producing at the same time), it yields a weekly output of 20,000 pots for that center. Enough to provide cooking wares to the whole region. Each potter works in his patio or in front of the house, and has his own place for firing, in the yard or a field nearby. Firing is done in two hours, on the ground , covered with cow dung. As the atmosphere is oxidizing in such open firing, the pots turn red (52).

51 Paddles with grooves for decoration, plain ones for building the pot. Half of a decorated pot can be seen right next to the paddles.

52 Potter Florencio Alejandro Alvites Valdez and his wife Flor Marina Tanta Sánchez from Mangallpa, with a stack of cooking pots ready to be sold at the market of San Pablo, the town in the valley three hours away below by foot.

53 Potter Santos Tanta Sánchez Mendoza (with red cap), his family and a helper. He is loading clay he just extracted and sieved from a field 15 minutes from his home. The material added as temper is a volcanic pyroclastic sand also found close by.

54 One of the extraction places for the volcanic temper used in the production of Mangallpa ceramics. These pits are half an hour away from the workshop (and home) of the potters. The whole area offers good clay and volcanic materials that are mined by all potters from Mangallpa. Other small extraction places are reported on the other side of the mountain used by a few potters from other communities. Judging by the similarity in body composition between archaeological ceramics and modern ones, these materials and the area was also mined in ancient times.

55 The clay is obtained from different fields. The potters often have to pay the owner to get their material.

56 Sr. Hernandez in his patio. He stopped producing many years ago. He couldn't afford to travel back to the quarry he knew before he moved some five hours away by foot.

57a Clay mold and the pot made with it (57b). Note the repair tie on the neck of the mold. Reproduced from Druc 2011, fig. 15, with permission from the Institut Français d'Etudes Andines.

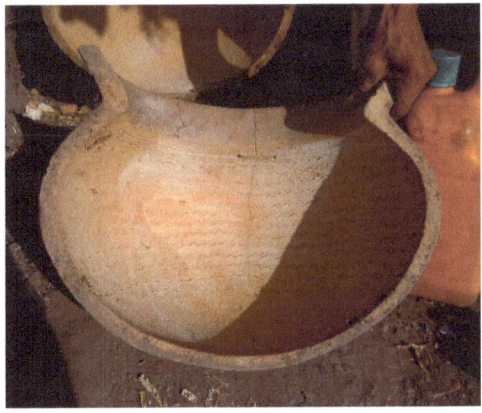

57a

57b

Potter Manuel Hernandez Suarez, in Cerro Blanco near San Pablo, Cajamarca, used to produce with bivalve molds that his father made. He is following the tradition of San Miguel de Pallaques and Jangala where his family is from. This tradition is different from the Mangallpa one, even though the two areas are only 16 km apart. Incisions on the inside of the molds leave a decoration in relief on the exterior surface of the wares when unmolded. However, the raw materials used (clay and volcanic sand) are similar for both traditions. When asked, the potters from each community say they would not know how the produce the way the 'others' do. The force of tradition is strong.

58

Children returning from school (58) and adobe bricks drying up (59). The quality of the clay and recipe for bricks are different than for pots, using coarser material and adding straw. The dry season is also the time for clay extraction and for traveling, as the roads are not slippery.

59

Potters of the Andes 37

60

Material ready to be used (60) by a Jangala potter, a small village 2500 m high in the Department of Cajamarca, Peru. His wife (62) is showing us how fine is the clay when sieved (61). He gets his clay 500 m from his home.

61

62

Potters of Cajamarca City

Cajamarca is a famous city in the north of Peru, where the last Inca emperor was captured by the Spaniards. The city is beautiful, prosperous, set at an elevation of 2750 m. It has an old colonial center (63, 64), and a few neighborhoods where you can find potters producing for the local and national markets. It is also the home of ceramist Lorenzo Cabrera Abanto, expert in reproducing the master pieces of the ancient cultures of Peru.

63

64

65 Ceramica Manya, workshop, outlet, and home of the Manya family, Cruz Blanca, Cajamarca city.

Manuel Manya Aquino (66), 22 at time of picture, with 7 years of practice, is a ceramist in Cruz Blanca, at the exit of the city. His family produces decorated jars and plates for the urban and tourist markets, as well as cooking pots (the red wares with lid) made with bivalve molds (67). His father and grandfather used to produce rustic wares, but the tourist market is a better venue now. Decorated ware can be produced with the kick wheel, by hand or with molds. The materials are often different than for traditional wares, finer and from different sources. The firing is done in a closed wood or electric kiln, rather than on the ground or in open kilns like those used for rustic ware.

68 The Mollepampa neighborhood where many potters live and work. In the background, one can see the city of Cajamarca.

69 Clay drying in the sun in the street, in front of a potter's house and workshop.

70 Stacks of cooking pots ready to be brought to the market. Middlemen take care of the distribution and a truck will come later to pick up the pots. The Cajamarca wares are famous for their cooking qualities and are sold in big and small cities throughout Peru.

Potters of the Andes 41

71

As most potters from Mollepampa in the outskirts of Cajamarca city, the family of Manuel Ocas Heras and Felicita Aquino Minchan produces cooking pots of small, medium and large sizes, using bivable molds (71-77).

72

73

42   Potters of the Andes

74

75

76

The potters of Mollepampa shifted from paddle-and-anvil to mold (77) some 30 years ago to speed up production. A mechanic grinder is now used and wares are fired with wood in a brick kiln(78). However, the ingredients are the traditional ones, a mix of two clay soils. One is found 15 minutes away, the other two hours away. Bivalve molds are used and the clay mixture is hand pressed into them. The molds are joined and left to dry, then the wares are unmolded. A slip is applied and the ware is briefly polished. The Ocas family can produce 100 small cooking pots, 60 medium or 12 large ones a day. In 2010, a small pot was sold the equivalent of 60 cents of a dollar or less, depending if it was sold with or without middlemen.

77

The Ocas family has two brick kilns to augment production output. They are fired with eucalyptus wood fed into the lower chamber. The firing first starts slowly for one hour, then the heat is allowed to build for three hours until maximum temperature is reached. The pots are let to cool down before unloading the kiln (78).

78

Sr Lorenzo Cabrera Abanto is a ceramist in Cajamarca. By personal interest he specialized in the reproduction of ancient Andean ceramics, as well as decorative wares, by experimenting with materials, firing conditions and temperatures to obtain the best replicas possible. 40 years ago he acquired a large quantity of the best clay around, which he stored in his workshop and has been using it ever since. He operates a large workshop away from his home and has an assistant. He refines his clay in decanting tanks for several weeks to months alternating this with time using a electric clay mixer to get the finest material. He manufactures his pieces using a slip-casting method, which allows for multiple reproductions of the same piece, and fires them in a wood kiln.

79 Sr. Cabrera, 78 in 2010. A pail of manganese powder to blacken the surface of some pieces lays in front, molds stack the wall of his workshop.

80 Some of Sr. Cabrera's replicas of ancient Andean ceramics. Reproduced from Druc 2011, fig. 10b, with permission from the Institut Français d'Etudes Andines.

81 Ceramist Angel Tamay Vargas, 78 in 2012, works in Trujillo, a coastal town in northern Peru, but he gets his clay from Cajamarca, 120 km away. The clay there is better than the local one, he says. He mixes it with local sand and uses molds to produce copies of the famous Moche and Chimu wares of northern Peru. He fires his wares with wood in an open kiln. Molding was already a feat known to the Moche (AD 200-600). His father was a potter too, producing replicas with local clays. He recalls him telling about the highland potters who used to come with their material to produce in the area.

Sr. Tamay Vargas has a small stand within the enclosure of the archaeological site of *Huaca Arco Iris* in Trujillo, a pre-Inca ceremonial center. He works there and offers his copies to the site visitors (82). Below the counter, we can observe stacks of molds and bags of prepared clay waiting to be used (83).

Further reading

Arnold, D. 1993. *Ecology and ceramic production in an Andean community.* Cambridge University Press, Cambridge.

Chavez, Karen L. Mohr 1992. The organization of production and distribution of traditional pottery in South Highland Peru. In *Ceramic production and distribution*, G.J. Bey III and C.A. Pool (eds), pp. 49-92. Westview Press, Boulder.

Druc, Isabelle. 2000. Shashal o no shashal. Esa es la cuestión. *Bulletin de l'Institut Francais d'Etudes Andines* 30(1): 157-173.

2001. Soil Sources for Ceramic Production in the Andes. In *Archaeology and Clays*, I. Druc (ed.), pp. 95-105. British Archaeological Reports S942. Adrian Books, Oxford.

2005. *Producción cerámica y etnoarqueología en Conchucos, Ancash, Perú.* Instituto Runa, Lima.

2011. Tradiciones alfareras del valle de Cajamarca y cuenca alta del Jequetepeque, Perú. *Bulletin de l'Institut Francais d'Etudes Andines* 40(2): 307-331.

2013. What is local? Looking at ceramic production in the Peruvian Highlands and beyond. Journal of Anthropological Research 69: 485-513.

Mackey, Carol and Maria Louise Sidoroff. 1998. A modern craftsman re-creates Peru's past pottery. *Bulletin of Primitive Technology* 15.

Olivas Weston, Marcela. 2003. A*rte popular de Cajamarca.* Antares, Artes y Letras, Lima.

Ramón, Gabriel. 2011. The swallow potters: itinerant technical styles in the Andes, in *Archaeological Ceramics: A Review of Current Research.* Simona Scarcella (ed.), pp. 160-175. BAR International Series 2193. Archaeopress, Oxford.

Roddick, Andrew and Elizabeth Klarich. 2013. *Arcillas* and *Alfareros*: Clay and temper mining practices in the Lake Titicaca Basin. In *Mining and Quarrying in the Ancient Andes*, N. Tripcevich and K.J. Vaughn (eds), pp. 99-122. Springer, New York.

Sillar, Bill. 2000. *Shaping Culture. Making pots and constructing households. An ethnoarchaeological study of pottery production, trade and use in the Andes.* BAR international series 883, Oxford.

Videos

Druc, Isabelle. 2006. *Andean potters of Conchucos.* https://vimeo.com/35529198.

2012. *Paddle-and-anvil technique, ceramic production in Mangallpa Peru.* https://vimeo.com/55308616.

2012.*Producción e itinerancia, entrevista con un alfarero tradicional de Ancash, Perú.* https://vimeo.com/42793251.

2012. *Ceramic production in Tarica, Peru.* https://vimeo.com/42790326.

3 Potters of Argentina

In Argentina and Chile, the traditional potters producing utilitarian wares are very few in comparison with Peru, Bolivia or Ecuador. 'The grandfathers' (*los abuelos*), how the old potters are referred to, have stopped producing or have passed away. Except in a few places, notably in southern Chile among Mapuche Indians or in northwest Argentina, the tradition has given way to modern techniques and styles taught in art schools and studios. In northern Chile people in the villages do not replace their earthenware pots once broken. This is changing, however, as interest in what is traditional is picking up again and is seen as a profitable market. Many ceramists now are trying to revive the ancient traditions, exploring the forms, decorations, materials, and types of open air firing allowing them to imitate the original techniques. One potter I was able to meet and who is still carrying the tradition is Atilio López (84) in the Andean piemont of western Argentina (85, 86). That is, the tradition before industrialization changed the way ceramic is produced and one in this case that reflects the cross of European and Amerindian ceramic making traditions, both in terms of manufacture and forms produced.

84

48   Potters of Argentina

85 Wikimedia map, 2011, by Bleff, Creative Commons, free documentation license.

86 Entrance to Atilio López' place.

Atilio López works year round and produces earthenware by hand, using coiling and pinching techniques with local materials (88-93). He learned how to make pots from his mother, helping her since he was seven, polishing wares and other jobs. His great-grandparents were of Spanish descent, his parents are '*criollos*', locals, possibly with some Comechingone Indian blood. Ceramic manufacture was an Indian traditional craft in the region, except that the Comechingone potters used the clay as found bordering the rivers, without decanting it, says Atilio, nor did they polish their pots. This is contrary to the Indian groups further north who produced more pottery and of better quality. Atilio still lives in his parents' house, where he was born, in Mina Clavero in the Andean foothills west of Cordoba. He produces utilitarian wares (frying and cooking pots, jars, bowls, etc.) and decorative pieces with traditional forms and motifs. These are inspired from the Amerindian repertoire (in red, top shelf of figure 87) as well as colonial and '*gaucho*' styles, like the little black riding boots with spurs (87) and bells (98). Atilio regularly demonstrates traditional production to school children and at regional craft events. He has won awards for his dedication to the trade and the quality of his pots.

87

As is often the case for isolated producers, the local clays he mines are found in small deposits, in layers 10-15 centimeters thick one meter below the ground surface. The clay is of variable quality and color. The deposits are 15 km away from his home, and he goes there by horse or bus. When clay is abundant, in large deposits, a community of potters is often established and a whole industry can develop as seen earlier in the case of Mangallpa or Mollepampa in Peru. Traditional potters may spend the whole day to get clay, looking for the right type. Some look fine at first, but do not withstand the firing, so experiments must be conducted. Atilio pays the owner of the field where the clay is. When too plastic or too sandy, the materials need to be modified, either by mixing different clays together or by refining the material. He refines his clay by decantation, in successive tanks of water (94a,b), a task his parents were not doing.

50 Potters of Argentina

89

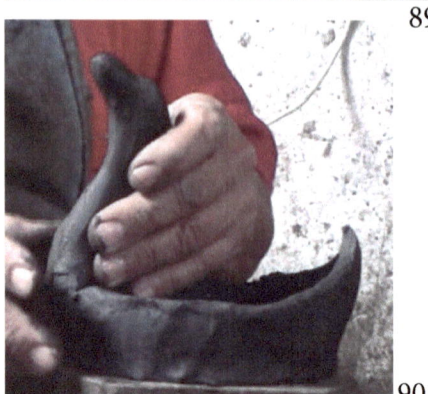

90

91

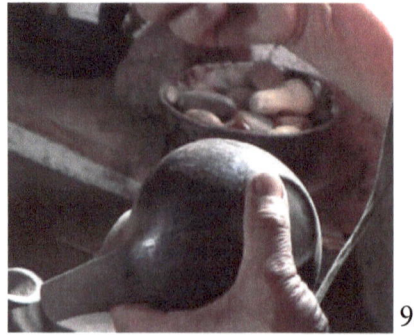

92

88

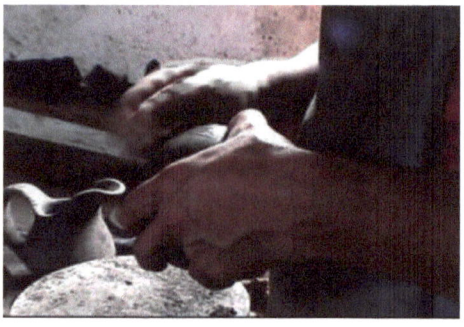

93

The wares are made, left to dry in the shade, scraped with a knife to remove all roughness, and smoothen with emery paper. Sr. López passes a damp cloth or sponge over the suface and polishes it carefully with a river pebble to achieve a metallic shine. Family members help with clay preparation or polishing. To produce pots of similar size, he uses a ruler to check the height and diameter.

88-93 Atilio López in his workshop, in Mina Clavero, Argentina, in 2001.

Potters of Argentina 51

94a

94b

94a-b Decanting clay to eliminate impurities.

95 A pot made by Atilio's parents with a coarse unrefined clay paste (96) and the fine body Atilio obtains with decantation (97, jar cross section).

95

96

97

The color red or black of Atilio's pieces results from the type of clay used, but also comes from the firing atmosphere, oxidized or reduced. Big pieces are fired in a small open kiln with a few containing rows of stones and bricks. Wood lays at the bottom and the wares are covered with cow dung. This type of firing takes two to three hours. He also uses a two-chamber brick kiln, which allows a slower, more controlled firing. He fires it with wood and gets temperatures of 900 to 950 degrees C. The smoke of the firing is often a reason why potters live in the outskirts of a city or village, as town people do not like it, says Atilio, echoing other potters. He fires 100-200 pieces a time, every month or less depending the demand. His customers are owners of craft shops in Cordoba, Mendoza, and Buenos Aires, as well as tourists who come to the area. When his mother was working 50 years ago, the demand was different, geared towards big water jars and cooking *braseros*, as well as decorative pots. A crew from the Art Department at the University of Cordoba filmed Atilio´s parents Alcira and Jesús Tómas López at work in 1965. In this great black and white documentary we see his father getting his horse to look for clay in the ravines near the river, and his mother forming a pot by hand. His father also manufactured pots.

98 Atilio López in 2012, proud of the metal-like polish and clear ring he achieved with the bell in his hands, proof of good workmanship and firing.

Further reading and videos

Concha S., Claudia. 1994. *Quinchamalí, cultura urdida entre gredas, arados y cerezos*. Taller de acción cultural, Santiago.

Cremonte, Maria Beatriz. 1988-1989. Técnicas alfareras tradicionales en la Puna: IntiCancha. *Arqueología Contemporánea* 2: 5-26.

Druc, Isabelle. 2012. *Atilio López, alfarero tradicional de la sierra argentina*. https://vimeo.com/97191953.

Gleyzer, Raymundo, Ana Montes de Gonzales and Escuela de Artes. 1965. *Ceramiqueros de Traslasierra*. Universidad Nacional de Córdoba, Cordoba.

Rex González, Alberto. 2007 (2nd ed). *Arte, estructura y arqueología*. La Marca, Buenos Aires.

Serrano, Antonio. 1958. *Manual de la cerámica indígena*. Editorial Assandri, Cordoba.

Varela, V. G. 2002. Learning from the Toconceños pottery makers: Ceramic tradition and technology. *Chungara* 34(1): 225-252. (In Spanish)

4 Potters of Mexico

99 Unpacking cooking vessels and plates at the market of Tonala, Jalisco, a major ceramic production center in central Mexico since pre-Hispanic times.

Mexico is home to many traditional potting communities, beside the big industrial factories manufacturing mayolica and the famous colorful Puebla ceramics sold world wide. The long ceramic traditions, Pre-hispanic and Hispanic, are a reflection of a very active craft industry. Utilitarian earthenware is very common, found in all the town's markets. They are still much used, but less publicized than the highly decorated glazed ware tourists are familiar with. The work of these crafstmen is illustrated here with the potters of San Marcos Acteopan, a small ceramic production village in the State of Puebla in east-central Mexico. These potters produce jars, cooking pots, pans and bowls, working year round, even during the rainy season from June to September, however less intensively during this time. The village borders the state of Morelos and is part of a nine-village parish founded in 1888. Acteopan is said to date to the 17th c. and was home to some 900 inhabitants in 1996. Six other villages in the Parish produce ceramics and are all reputed for their fire-resistant wares. Each specializes in producing a particular range of utilitarian vessels, ornamental ceramics and water fountains.

In San Marcos Acteopan, the brothers Evaristo and Valente Torres Bravo and their families share a ceramic business and a kiln. Usually the tradition is taught from parents to children, however, the two brothers learned by watching neighbors manufacturing pots. Because they used to accompany their father for trading trips to Taxco, in the neighboring state of Guerrero, they started selling their wares in this town, benefitting from being the only potters from their village to do so.

54 Potters of Mexico

100 Map of Mexico released into public domain by its author Alex Covarrubias. Modified to highlight the States mentioned in the text.

101 Evaristo's wares sold in the market of Taxco, Guerrero, three hours and a half away by car from San Marcos Acteopan.

102

Brigida, the oldest daughter of Evaristo and Ignacia demonstrating how the clay is pounded and sieved.

103

One interesting aspect of the production in San Marcos Acteopan is the way they prepare the raw material. The potters only use one type of clay, a yellow one, which they mine and buy from another village in the Parish, 20 minutes away by truck. They may also buy it from providers coming to the village with truckloads of clay. The clay is pounded, one part is sieved, the other is decanted in a tub with water so as to separate the heavy particles, small mineral grains and plant impurities from the finer clay materials. The solution is sieved and the coarse material thrown away. The clay slurry is then remixed with the dry, sieved material, which contains clay and sand-size grains. This way, the potters control the proportion of clay slurry and dry material and obtain a better texture in relation to the type of ware to produce. The clay paste is prepared each morning, in enough quantity to produce some 40 pots.

104

105

Men and women participate in the production. In the Torres Bravo family, husband and wife work as a team. One prepares the clay '*tortilla*' that will be wraped over the mold, the other rolls a clay coil that will be used to make the rim of the cooking pot (104, 105). The coil is added after the bottom part has dried a little. Then handles are added.

Evaristo and Ignacia have two daughters and one son. The children also help, cleaning the pots, polishing, moving them out of the sun. Too much sun can damage the wares, which can dry too quickly and crack. Children begin helping at age 11 or 12, and start making pots at 15 years old.

106

107

The Torres brothers built their own brick kiln (106, 107). Firing is done with wood that is acquired from traders from another village in the Parish who specialize in getting wood for potters. It takes 4 to 5 days of work to have enough pots to fire. The firing is done in two stages. First, the pots are fired two hours to obtain a biscuit. The wares are then let to cool, rubbed and dipped into a lead-base glaze. To melt the glaze onto the surface, a second firing is required. This one takes nearly three hours and is done with guayaba wood, which does not smoke and can produce high kiln temperatures. Applying a glaze is said to prevent the food from sticking to the pan. When applied on the outside surface, the potters say that it offers a better resistance to flames when cooking (and it is attractive). Lead paint or glaze was widely used in Mexico until recently. Known to be unhealthy, potters are now switching to other glazes.

Mayan art and its reproduction

Alfredo González Castillo is a master ceramist and sculptor reproducing ancient pieces from Mexico's cultural heritage. "One has to respect the lines and the culture" says Alfredo Gonzáles in an interview I had with him in 2007. After years in Mexico City, he returned to his native Yucatan and lives in a small traditional house, in the village of Francisco Uh May along the road between the coastal city of Tulum and the famous archaeological site of Coba, in the State of Quintana Roo.

108 Alfredo González Castillo in his workshop in 2011.

Don Alfredo has been experimenting with local clays, decorating slips and firing to reproduce what the ancient potters had achieved (109). He knows about geology and chemistry, reads several languages, and has an incredible mastery of his art that he has been teaching for 30 years to his sons, Glenn and Eric Gonzáles Licona.

Potters of Mexico 59

With his two sons, and more particularly Glenn, he produces exact replicas of ancient art pieces, true to the slightest details and dimensions. They copy museum pieces or decorated Maya vases published in archaeology books. The wares are all handbuilt, modeled or turned on a small table wheel that is also used to decorate the pieces.

110 Replica of a Maya vase based on an illustration in Michael Coe's book (1973).

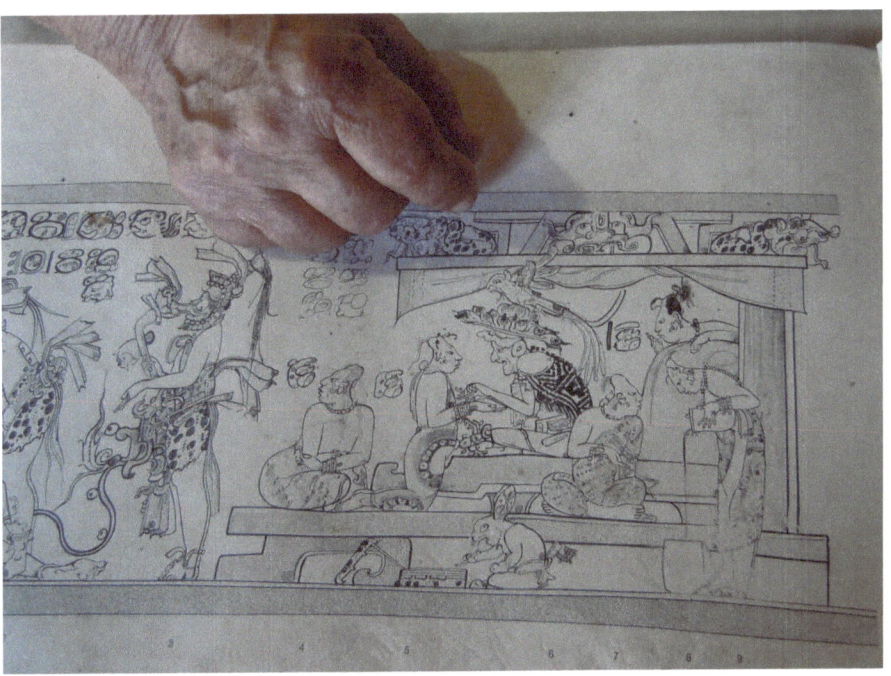

111 Roll-out from an ancient Maya vase design published in Michael Coe's book.

His brother Wilbert Gonzáles founded in 1972 a school, cooperative and Maya Indian Art factory in Ticul, Yucatan. He was an excellent artist, featured in Kelker and Bruhns book (2010, 71-72). His sister Lourdes Castillo is also a famous painter of Mayan art. It runs in the family. The pieces Don Alfredo and his suns produce are carefully crafted, carved, painted, polished, and even aged if necessary. Alfredo Gonzáles does not sign his pieces. He states that the artists are the Mayas, not him, and he only sells his pieces as replicas. The problem arises when these pieces are resold as originals.

112 Alfredo Gonzáles Castillo exhibits an award he received in Mexico. He also won an international competition of art in Munich, Germany.

113 A few of Alfredo Gonzáles' sculptures and reproductions.

114 Kiln used by Alfredo Gonzales and his sons to fire their pieces. The kiln is covered with lime and gypsum and the wares are fired with wood to temperatures between 800 and 900 degrees or slightly more. To obtain the black color of certain reproductions, Don Alfredo submits them to a reduction process by putting the hot pieces in wood shavings. This induces oxygen deprivation and a chemical reaction leading to iron reduction causing the surface to turn black.

115 Alfredo Gonzáles Castillo's workshop.

Further reading

Arnold, Dean E. 1978. The ethnography of pottery making in the Valley of Guatemala. In *The ceramics of Kaminaljuyu*, R. Wetheringtonz (ed.), pp. 327-400. The Pennsylvania State University Press, University Park. 2008. *Social change and the evolution of ceramic production and distribution in a Maya community*. University Press of Colorado, Boulder.

Arnold, Philip J., III. 1991. *Domestic Ceramic Production and Spatial Organization: A Mexican Case Study in Ethnoarchaeology*. Cambridge University Press, Cambridge.

Coe, Michael. 1973. *The Maya Scribe and his world*. Grolier Club, New York.

Deal, Michael. 1998. *Pottery Ethnoarchaeology in the Central Maya Highlands*. University of Utah Press, Salt Lake City.

Druc, Isabelle. 2000. Ceramic production in San Marcos Acteopan, Puebla, Mexico. *Ancient Mesoamerica* 11: 77-89.

Kaplan, Flora. *A Mexican folk pottery tradition: cognition and style in material culture in the Valley of Puebla*. Southern Illinois University Press, Carbondale.

Kelker, Nancy L. and Karen O. Bruhns. 2010. *Faking Ancient Mesoamerica*. Left Coast Press, Walnut Creek CA.

Lackey, Louana. 1989. *The pottery of Acatlan*. University of Oklahoma Press, Norman.

Pool, C. A. 2000. Why a kiln? Firing technology in the Sierra de los Tuxtlas, Veracruz (Mexico). *Archaeometry* 42: 61–76.

Reina, Ruben, and Robert Hill. 1978. *The traditional pottery of Guaatemala*. University of Austen Press, Austen.

Videos

Druc, Isabelle. 2010. *El arte Maya según Alfredo Gonzáles Castillo*. https://vimeo.com/35601782.

2010. *Arte Prehispánico. Entrevista con Eric Gonzáles Licona*. https://vimeo.com/35569127.

5 Potters of Turkey

In Turkey, two very different ceramic traditions can be found. One relates to the porcelain-like wares called *çini* (pronounced 'cheenee') produced on the wheel by men. These are fine, decorated and glazed pieces. They became in fashion during Ottoman times from the 14th to the late 18th hundreds and are much in demand now. *Çini* is usually produced on the wheel by men. The other tradition is that of earthenware production of cooking pots and domestic ware, handbuilt by female potters. They are still produced in several Anatolian villages. In addition, as elsewhere, there are ceramic artists who bring the art of ceramic making to the spotlight. Güngör Güner is one of them, with her avant-garde pieces. She is also the first scholar (she is a professor at Marmara University, Istanbul) to have written a detailed account of traditional ceramic production in Turkey. Ayşegül Özen Türedi, in Eskişehir, is another female ceramic artist and professor, who gets her inspiration from traditional earthenware production and who wrote another important and well illustrated book on the topic. Murat Ires (119) is a ceramic artist in Istanbul, now specialized in reproducing classical Ottoman wares, at which he excels.

116 Earthenware production in Sorkun, Anatolia.

117 Wikimedia map, Turkey relief location map by Turkey_location_map.svg: Nord NordWest derivative work: Uwe Dedering (talk). Licensed under CC BY-SA 3.0 via Wikimedia Commons - https://commons.wikimedia.org/wiki/, modified by the author to show sites mentioned in the text.

118a

118b

Creation (118a) and reproductions (118b-c) of Ottoman wares by ceramist Murat Ires, Istanbul.

118c

Murat Ires experimented with different materials and firing conditions to be as close to the originals as possible. Art collectors and museum seek his pieces, which he signs by a stamp, Ottoman style. To obtain the black color proper to Ottoman reduced wares, he built his firing box with his son, a mechanical engineer. He experimented with various temperatures and the right amount of wood shavings to burn. Reduction firing is a combustion process by which the surface and sometimes the body of a ware turns black due to carbon deposits and a change in the state of the iron compounds present in the clay to a reduced or less oxidized form. The firing box is built limiting the access of oxygen, hence creating a reducing atmosphere. If oxygen access is not limited, like in an open kiln, the firing happens in an oxidizing atmosphere and the wares become reddish or light in color, as the iron naturally present in the clay stays oxidized. Murat also has an electric kiln in his workshop, where the red pieces shown here were fired.

Temperature is an important factor needed to reach proper ceramic body and surface color. Murat Ires monitors the temperature using thermocouples. Studio potters and ceramic artists also often use temperature cones. Traditional potters however usually know when a pot is ready or when it is time to stop feeding the fire by looking at the flames, or the color of the pots in the fire. It is often necessary to let the pots cool before removing them from the kiln to avoid a thermal shock that could cause the pieces to crack.

A glaze or decoration under the glaze may be applied on the biscuit ware, which is then refired. Biscuits are ceramic pieces fired once, usually at temperatures of 1000-1040 degrees. This first firing, usually in an oxidizing atmosphere, transforms the clay ware into a hard, but porous material. The second firing will fix or melt the glaze onto the surface. Çini ware is made in this way, in addition to requiring a special clay and firing temperature.

119 Murat Ires in his workshop in Üsküdar, Istanbul.

120 Ceramic tile from Iznik decorating the inside walls of Rüstem Pasha Mosque in Istanbul, XVI century.

121 *Çini* plate from Zide workshop in Iznik.

122 Stacking bowls in a kiln for biscuit firing. The firing takes six hours, reaching temperatures of 1000 to 1100 degrees C. The wares are then left to cool for 24 hours, and only then is the oven opened.

123

Çini production in Kütahya

Çini tiles (120) used to ornate mosques, basins, fountains, palaces and the wares were in high demand in Ottoman times. Iznik, 100 km southeast of Istanbul, was the capital of çini production during the 14th and 17th centuries. After the decline of production there, Kütahya took over as main production center.

In large ceramic production centers, the work is often subdivided into specialized tasks carried out by different individuals in separate workshops or areas of a factory. These workshops do only some steps of the manufacture. Artisans are subcontracted or independant. In the case of Hasan Efe and Mehmet Ali in Kütahya (124, 125), they buy the biscuit wares (pre-fired plain wares) from Ertuğrul Çini, a small factory owned by Ertuğrul Bey in Kütahya. They decorate them in their studio (123-125) and bring the pieces back to the factory where the second firing takes place to fix the decoration and glaze. At Ertuğrul Çini, several artisans work as employees or associates. There are two turners, one person at the kiln, the owner who oversees the whole production business, ten decorators working in five different workshops, and five shops to sell the wares in Istanbul.

Hasan Efe and Mehmet Ali decorate *çini* ware and sell the finished products at their shop in one of the new malls on the outskirts of town where national and foreign tourists stop regularly. They have been working at this for 15 years.

Inspiration comes from traditional motifs and art books. The design is traced and transferred onto the surface with charcoal and lines are drawn. The decor is then painted with decorating colorants that will melt into the glazes. This type of ware is in high demand throughout the country and abroad.

124

125

126 A turner at Ertuğrul Çini workshop in Kütahya, western Turkey.

127

128

A turner can produced 200 pieces a day. Products are standardized. To ensure equal form, thickness and bottom design, jigger and jolley templates are used to shape the inside and outside profiles of the vessels. Here (127) the turner shapes the plate on a plaster mold, then uses a jigger (128) to shape the bottom of the plate. Each plate size requires a different mold and template. However, the thickness of the plate depends upon the pressure exercised by the potter on the lever while the wheel is turning. Expertise and years of work are needed to obtain uniformity.

Earthenware production in Sorkun

In many countries, as in Turkey, the use of the wheel is often the realm of the men, while women work with handbuilding techniques. One of the reasons for this gender division of labor is linked to the domestic and family tasks a woman needs to perform that interrupt craft production, be it textile, basket making or ceramics. Men, on the contrary, can dedicate themselves to intensive production and work in workshops and factories separated from home.

Earthenware production in Turkey is illustrated by the work of the women potters of Sorkun, a small village of some 500 people in central Anatolia. In 2007, 150 families were involved in *çömlek* (earthen pot) production. Besides potato farming and sheep herding, men may help with ceramic production, getting the material and preparing it or involved in some other steps of the production like at Osman and Firdevs Sert family, featured below.

129

The village of Sorkun (129, 130) is located midway between Ankara, the capital of Turkey, and the town of Eskişehir, 125 km northeast of that town. The houses are built of stone and mud mortar, are two stories tall, and have a courtyard and a barn for sheep, goats and cows.

The wares are produced with a micaceous clay material mined from neighboring rock outcrops with very high schistosity, called *ak toprak* (white-clean soil) of blue, white, green or yellow color. A red soil called *kızıl toprak* is also dug out from fields about one kilometer away from the village. The proportion for the body is two measures of white soil for one of red soil (2:1), although this may slightly change according to the composition of the red soil. The latter is dug at depths of three to five meters in Aßılık and Kocakızıllık, while the white soil is mined from the Tilkiinligi, Kabaçam and Tuzla rocks and in the area of Emirçam. An interesting point is the use of the word *toprak* (soil) and not *kil* (clay), leaving that denomination to the purer material used for the production of *çini*.

The red soil is crushed and sieved, and combined with hot water to remove undesired inclusions, straw and small stones. The women (and often men too) prepare the clay body, called *çamur*, mixing the soils with water and tramping it for a full day to mix it homogeneously. The resulting paste is then left to mature a few days.

While firing is usually limited to the warmer months of the year, May/June to September/October, production goes on during the rest of the year, at a slower pace. The wares are dried and stocked inside their homes until the weather allows for firing.

130

Gülsüm (131-132) was 42 years old at the time of my visit. She has three boys and had been producing *çömlek* since she was 15. She started learning and helping at age 12. Ten to twelve years old is the usual age to start learning the craft. With experience, a good potter produces about 10 large *çömlek* a day, 100 pots a week. The pots are produced on a 'tournette' (banding wheel), a simple elevated revolving plate that is turned by hand while working on the pot. A ceramic disc serves as plate upon which the piece is built.

A ball of clay is flattened to form the base, and coils are added to build the walls. A wooden spatula helps to push out the walls, scrape and smooth them. A cloth is used to smooth the surface. The building process takes about 12 minutes per pot. Here, Gülsüm was called inside so a neighbor finished her pot (133).

Potters of Turkey 73

134 Osman Sert pounding the raw material.

135 Tools for ceramic production in Sorkun. The spatula size is in relation to the size of the pot to produce.

136 Ceramic discs upon which the wares are built. In other villages, these plates can be large, thick and concave, and serve as turning table (see Güngör Güner 1988).

137 Nizamettin Arslan, a friend, shows how the white earth is sifted.

138 Osman and Firdevs Sert 'glazing' the wares with a micaceous slip.

The second step in the manufacture is the scraping of the dry surface with a metal blade or wood to remove roughness to smooth the outer surface. Then comes the application of a micaceous slip on the outer and inner surfaces of the wares. To do so, the air-dried pots are warmed around an open fire (138) and the slip is applied vigorously with a rag. This slip is made with white and red soils in proportion of 10 to 1, adding water only to reach a thick slurry. This coating is said to restrain the pots from swelling and to yield better, fire resistant wares. Osman and Firdevs Sert have been producing earthenware pots for more than 24 years and have no other income. They have five children, two boys and three girls (28, 26, 22, 20 and 11 years old in 2007). The last one helps when not at school. The family produces some 100 çömlek a week of different sizes.

139 Firing in Sorkun. Photograph kindly provided by Nizamettin Arslan.

140 Pots cooling down.

The wares are let to dry and wood fired later when the wind blows in the correct direction. This will allow the fire to burn fast, reaching temperatures of 600 to 700 degrees C. The pots are fired in two hours, on the ground at the outskirts of the village, a place used by all the potters (139, 140). A first row of pots is laid upside down upon a bed of straw and sawdust, followed by alternate layers of oak wood and pots arranged to form a large rectangle. The women are in charge of the firing and may be helped by their husbands. Many families also produce oblong fish pans and large round, flat bread pans. The small fish pans are fired stacked on top of each other while the flat bread pans are fired at home in the fireplaces or on outside open-air structures. Earthenware cooking pots, fish and bread pans are commonly used for cooking throughout Turkey.

A selling stand on the road near Ankara (141) and plastic jars offered by a street vendor in Beypazarı, Anatolia (142). The earthenware jar will keep the water cool, an advantage over a plastic container.

Further reading

Carswell, John. 2007. *Iznik pottery*. Interlink Books, Northampton, MA.

Glassie, Henry. 1993. *Turkish traditional art today*. Indiana University Press, Bloomington.

Güngör Güner. 1988. *Anadolu'da Yasamakta Olan Ilkel Çömlekçilik*. Akbank, Istanbul.

Özen, Ayşegül Türedi. 2001. *Geleneksel çömlek sanati*. Anadolu Üniversitesi, Eskişehir.

Videos

Druc, Isabelle. 2008. *Women potters of Sorkun, Turkey*. https://vimeo.com/35526032.

2008. *Murat Ires, master potter*. https://vimeo.com/35567360.

2008. *Reduction Firing. The creation of Ottoman Blackware by Potter Murat Ires*. https://vimeo.com/35532313.

2008. *Çini: The production of Kütahya's porcelain*. https://vimeo.com/35633427.

2010. *Bridging traditional and modern ceramic productions. Ayşegül Türedi Özen, ceramist*. https://vimeo.com/147801657.

Kircalioğlu, Neşet. 1985. *The legend of Uslu*. Kare film A.S. Turkey.

6 Potters of Thailand

Ceramic production in Thailand, as in many other parts of mainland Southeast Asia, has developed to a high level of organization and achievement, from earthenware, to stoneware, celadon and porcelain productions. Pottery is manufactured in different settings, which differ in context, concentration, scale, intensity, production area, number of persons involved, specialization, standardization, and for whom the wares are produced.

The village of Ban Muang Kung, 10 km southwest of Chiang Mai in northern Thailand, illustrates how earthenware production is organized in small, nucleated workshops and factories. Production occurs yearlong at a high intensity and is standardized. Not all production steps are carried out by the same person, and each has a specific task to perform. The wares are turned by hand or on an electric wheel and a wide range of utilitarian and decorative vessels are produced. The potters acquire clay from 30 km away by truck and only use one material.

143 Potter Par Pun starting the production of a jar. He flattens the base and will add coils to form the walls, lifting them on the electric wheel. He controls the height and diameter of the vessel with a measuring stick (146).

144 Wikimedia map, Creative Commons. Modified by the author to show sites in Thailand (Chiang Mai, Ban Muang Kung) and Vietnam (Bat Trang, Phu Lang) mentioned in the text.

145 Unfired pots drying in the factory of Mrs. Bualai, Ban Muang Kung.

146

147

Mr. Par Pun learned from his father and is now a well-accomplished potter. With his assistant, he can produce 20 big jars a day (148).

148

149

Par Pun built a two-chamber kiln, and fires it with wood. The firing above was started the night before and continued all day at c. 1000 degrees C. It will require one day to cool down.

150 House and workshop of Par Pun, Ban Muang Kung.

151 One of the two kilns at Mrs. Bualai factory, Ban Muang Kung. Firing typically takes about 8 hours at 800 to 1000 degrees C. according to the size of the pots.

82 Potters of Thailand

152

The production in Mrs Bualai's factory in Ban Muang Kung is divided by tasks and carried on in different parts of the compound. As in many other parts of Thailand, men usually turn the pieces on the electric wheel (152) while the women produce smaller pieces on a tournette (153, 156), decorate, polish or coat the wares. The polishing is done with a smooth pebble and gasoline (154, 155).

153

154

155

Potters of Thailand 83

156 Pots formed on a tournette in a small workshop.

157 Wares drying in the alley in front of the workshop.

158 Wares can be blackened by smudging them in hot ashes. This produces a reduction reaction and the surface of the ware turns black. Mrs Bualai's factory, Ban Muang Kung.

Thailand, as other Southeastern Asian countries, is also famous for the production of celadon ware. Celadon is a high-fired product requiring kilns able to reach temperatures between 1260 and 1300 degrees C. in a reducing atmosphere. It has a characteristic pale to dark green color (161) and the term can refer to a glaze or the whole vessel. Below is an example of a small celadon factory in Chiang Mai: Baan Celadon (159-163). The factory also has a showroom and sales department geared toward the tourist market. The work is realized in different areas according to the steps of production, and specialists operate as salaried workers. Celadon ware is high priced and much valued. The wares are turned or slip-cast (159), then glazed , and over glaze colors can be painted on a piece (162) before firing.

159 Taking off a plaster mold to expose the cast bowl.

160 Glazed, unfired ceramics.

Potters of Thailand 85

161 Celadon wares once fired, displaying their true color.

162 Decorating a glazed, unfired vase.

163 Fired products on display.

164   Small shrine in Ban Muang Kung, Thailand.

Further reading

Cort, Louise Allison and Leedom Lefferts. 2005. Not primitive, certainly not simple: Women's earthenware production in Mainland Southeast Asia. *The Journal of the Asian Arts Society of Australia* 14(4): 7-9.

2012. Pots and how they are made in Mainland Southeast Asia. *Transactions of the Oriental Ceramic Society* 75, 2010-2011: 1-16.

Lefferts, Leedom and Louise A. Cort. 2003. A preliminary cultural geography of contemporary village-based earthenware production in Mainland Southeast Asia, in *Earthenware in Southeast Asia*, J. Miksic (ed): 300-310. Singapore University Press, Singapore.

Rooney, Dawn 1987. *Folk pottery in South-East Asia*. Oxford University Press, Singapore.

1984. *Khmer ceramics*.Oxford University Press, Singapore.

Shippen, Mick. 2005. *The traditional ceramics of Southeast Asia*. University of Hawaii Press, Hawaii.

Underhill, Anne. 2003. Investigating variation in organization of ceramic production: An ethnoarchaeological study in Guizhou, China. *Journal of Archaeological Method and Theory* 10(3): 203-275.

7 Potters of Vietnam

165 Bringing pots to the kiln. Note the piles of wood for firing the kiln.

Stoneware and porcelain productions in northern Vietnam

Craft production is organized at the village or neighborhood level in Vietnam. For ceramics, five centers are known within 60 km of Hanoi, the capital. Phu Lang (Bac Ninh province) and Bat Trang (in the outskirts of Hanoi) are two of them. One specializes in stoneware production, the other in high-fired ceramics and porcelain. Ceramic production in Phu Lang and Bat Trang dates back to the 14th century.

In Phu Lang, some 800 families are engaged in the trade. They produce small to very large jars, bowls, and cooking wares on the wheel. Small coffins are also manufactured with slabs and coils for the joints. The coffins are used for secondary burial of the bones of the deceased after three years of burial in a wooden coffin. Stoneware production in Phu Lang is qualified as a village industry, where independent specialists work in individual workshops usually attached to their home, manufacturing standardized products and forming a clustered community of practice. However, between 1954 after the revolution, and the early 1990s, craft production was organized in cooperatives and individual production was banned (Fanchette and Stedman 2009). This caused the decline of several craft villages and changes in the products manufactured. When the cooperatives closed the potters had to adapt to new markets and modern requirements.

166 Craft villages benefit from a location close to the river. This is the case for Phu Lang and Bat Trang. In ancient times it was the main axis for material transport and products distribution. Now, due to road access, trucks are used more than boats (167). Red clay from the Red River Delta acquired 25 km away is used to produce all the different stoneware products of Phu Lang.

167 Transporting clay in Phu Lang.

168 Workshop of Phạm Văn Nam (preparing coils) and Tran Thị Thanh (finishing up a coffin. The caskets are produced joining pressed clay slabs (169), consolidating the joints with coils at the bottom and top of the small rectangular box. To avoid the clay from sticking to the forms, they use rice hull ash (170). The forms are carved with dragon or other motifs that will appear in relief in the finish product. It takes five minutes to make a casket; 80 to 100 are produced in a day. The profit margin is slim, at five cents per casket.

170 Cleaning a form before starting over.

171 Yard of a retailer who will distribute the products to markets in other cities.

172 Phạm Văn Tình's workshop with Biển producing small cooking pots on the wheel. The initial step is a ball of clay, pounded and opened with the fist. Then the walls are turned, shaped out of that single ball. In the same workshop, concurrently and with the same clay, various products and ware sizes can be produced with different manufacturing techniques.

Learning the profession, with actual practice of wheel throwing starts around 14-15 year old, but the children observe and can be asked to help and produce smaller products when younger. Specializing in one technique or another is up to each person capabilities. However, it is usually the women who are forming the pots, while the men help with the heavy work and the production of the coffins. Men are also more involved in the firing process.

Local craft production has to compete with foreign trade but still offers a better income than agriculture (Fanchette and Stedman 2009, 37). Now that families are less numerous, with two children instead of five and more, work rely on the help of non-family members. Production is done on demand. Custom orders for private persons, restaurants and businesses are taken, often following specific instructions as to the style, shape, decoration, or ornamentation of the jar handles for example.

173 The potters combine two techniques when building big jars. Thick rings of clay coils are superposed on a flat clay-disc and pulled on the wheel while the jar is taking shape. Teams of two women usually work together, one preparing the coils, the other forming the pots. The jar above required 10 clay rings to build it. Two more rings will be added to finish the neck and rim. Workshop of Pham Vinh Toan and Truong Thị Tam, Phu Lang.

174 The tool in front of the pots has a wire at the base to cut the clay out of the clay pile. The rim of the jars are unglazed so they can be stacked without sticking when fired.

175 Pots cooling off inside the kiln and unfired pots drying on top. The grey color is a river mud and bamboo leave ash glaze that turns chocolate brown when fired. Another plant-based glaze turns green.

Potters of Vietnam 93

176, 177 House and workshop of Pham Vinh Toan and Trưởng Thị Tam, Phu Lang. The couple has three children, two of whom are girls studying at a university in Hanoi, one in business, the other in social studies. The third one, a boy, is only nine. The couple has won recognition for the excellence of their products.

178 Trưởng Thị Tam pulling the clay out of the mixer. Mixing the clay used to be done by foot, but the process became more mechanized and electric mixers and electric wheels are now used. Another change is the pigments and decoration added to the wares. The chocolate brown or green glazes are however traditional. The glaze is applied on the dry pieces and not on a biscuit, therefore only one firing is needed.

179 Stoneware jars, Phu Lang.

180

181

Production occurs year round but slows down during the rainy season June to end of September. The best period for firing is between October to December. Tunnel kilns (with several chambers) are used, that several families can fire. There are some 30 kilns in Phu Lang. To produce enough to fill a kiln, other potters can give a hand as an exchange of services or, more rarely, as paid labor. It can take up to two months to get the quantity of products needed for a firing.

In a kiln, the pots are stacked according to the heat needed: the closer to the firing chamber in the front, the higher the temperature, which can reach between 1100 to 1600 degrees C. Heat is distributed throughout the different chambers of the kiln by convection, uphill, as warm air passes from one chamber to the next to reach the chimney. The pots are stacked from the floor to the roof in different chambers according to type, size and temperature required. The position within the chamber is also important. Stacking a kiln is an art or a profession. There used to be teams and guilds for stacking, as well as for firing. It takes time and great care. Pots can easily crack if this is not well done. In contrast to porcelain or delicate ceramics, saggars (boxes to protect the pieces and insure even atmosphere) are not used for stoneware production.

The kiln is fed for two days (182), allowing the temperature to rise. After maximum temperature is achieved, stoking is stopped. All openings are closed and the kiln is left to cool down three to four days before opening it. Here again, care is required. Opening a kiln too soon could result in damages as cold air would produce a temperature shock and pieces could crack.

182

Ceramic production in Bat Trang, northeast of Hanoi, Vietnam

183 Protecting Bat Trang, this marble Buddha sits in front of the town shrine. Below (184) is the entrance to the communal house.

184

The ceramic village of Bat Trang focuses on porcelain production, traditional and innovative, as well as touristy. The town is close to Hanoi and has many shops oriented towards the tourist trade, both national and foreign. This ceramic center flourished during the 15th and later centuries in relation to the expansion of ancient Hanoi. To provide for the capital and take advantage of the excellent white clay resources there, potters were resettled in Bat Trang, a common practice in many countries.

In the past, Bat Trang potters would produce pieces for the religious needs as well as utilitarian products for the aristocracy, communal houses, pagodas, temples and common people. Patrons and customers place orders and workshops have secure distribution networks that extend well beyond the capital.

185

Production nowadays uses the slip casting technique for many of the pieces, allowing mass production. The slip is emptied in molds or casts, like the white two and three-pieces molds standing at the entrance of the workshop (186). With this technique, much storage space is needed.

186

To save drying time, the vases can be dried in a warm kiln, or with an electric bulb hanging inside the mold. Due to lack of space, workshops now use electric or box kilns. In Bat Trang box kilns are fired with wood and coal patties.

187 Vases cooling down in a box kiln.

Decorators (185, 188, 189) are hand painting the wares following traditional designs, applied directly onto the unfired vases. Glazes are then applied. Bat Trang ceramics are famous for the different glazes used, in particular its crackle glaze, which results from a difference of fit between the glaze to the clay body. The success of a glaze shows the expertise of a potter, requiring precision in measuring the ingredients, firing to the correct temperature, and application artistry.

188

189

In big workshops or factories, the work is carried out by different people for the manufacture, decoration and firing, sometimes even in different places in town. In Bat Trang, the preparation and mixing of the clay is centralized in a big factory (190).

To produce high-fired white ceramics, much care is taken in the preparation of the material, by breaking, sieving and purifying it in big tanks of water for weeks or months.

190 Clay preparation factory.

191 Mixing vat for slip casting clay (far right) and slip-cast molds with electric bulb hanging inside to speed up the drying process (front).

192 Transporting the slurry for slip casting from one workshop to another.

Potters of Vietnam   101

193

Bat Trang wares used to be fired in big multi-chambered kilns. One of these old dragon kilns (193) is now the destination of hundreds of school children to learn about traditional crafts (194). Present day firing methods for high fired ceramics -worldwide- resort to gas or electric kilns, or coal as in Bat Trang. The temperature can be monitored precisely and each workshop can own one. Furthermore, the quantity of wood necessary to fire those huge kilns is not cost-effective or available. In Phu Lang, wood firing in multi-chambered kilns is still the norm, however.

The type or number of kilns and their size also depends upon the economic level of the owner of the workshop or factory.

194

195 Stoneware gaskets, Phu Lang, Vietnam.

Further reading

Fanchette, Sylvie and Nicholas Stedman. 2009. *A la découverte des villages de métier au Vietnam. Dix itinéraires autour de Hanoi.* Institut de recherche pour le développement, Marseille.

Nguyễn Khác Viên. 1992. *Arts and Handicrafts of Vietnam.* The Gioi, Hanoi.

Phan Huy Lê, Nguyễn Quang Ngọc and Nguyễn Dình Chiến. 1995. *Bat Trang Ceramics. 14th-19th centuries.* The Gioi publishers, Hanoi.

Stevenson, John. 1997. The evolution of Vietnamese ceramics, in *Vietnamese Ceramics: A separate tradition*, J. Stevenson and J. Guy (eds), pp. 23-45. Art Media resources with Averi Press, Chicago.

Video

Druc, Isabelle. 2015. Phu Lang: A Ceramic Village in Northern Vietnam. https://vimeo.com/134255181

8 From the producer to the table

Once produced, the pieces go to the consumers. Markets, fairs, direct sales at the potter's shop, traders, stores, are all options in acquiring pottery. The photographs below illustrate part of the life of a pot beyond its production and some venues in which traditional wares are used.

Wares being prepared to be sent to the market.

196 Bat Trang, northern Vietnam.

197 Mollepampa, Cajamarca, Peru.

104　From the producer to the table

198　Transporting the finished products to a shop in town, Bat Trang, northern Vietnam. Potters may form a partnership with a vendor or own a store. In an old town like Bat Trang, many workshops are located in buildings in the old quarters and the streets are very narrow (190). Only a bike or motorbike can go through. If the wares are sent for distribution outside of town, the products will be packed well, and the loading point will be at the entrance of the town,

199

From the producer to the table   105

200 Unloading a pick-up truck full of cups for the Tonala market, Central Mexico.

201 A highland Andean market, where all kinds of products are sold. Note the tricycle with packed pots waiting to be unloaded.

202 Choosing the right cooking pot in the San Pablo weekly market, Cajamarca, Peru. The potter's wife (with the red sweater) is monitoring the sale. In the past it was very common to barter the products, and a pot was often worth its full content of cereal or other agricultural product. Cash sales are now usual, but many potters say bartering yields a better deal.

203 A market in Cuenca, Ecuador. Many producers come here to sell their wares. Some have a stand, others leave their products to a person in town in charge of this aspect of the trade.

204 A peddler selling aluminum pots in Bat Trang, Vietnam. This is quite a paradox for a town which is a ceramic production center. Plastic containers and aluminum pots are ubiquitous world around, and direct competitors to earthenwares and local pottery productions.

Shifting demand

Consumers' taste for aluminum pots has impacted traditional potters. The two photos below have been taken 16 years apart in 1997 and 2013. Nicanor Saavedra, from Tarica, Peru, used to produce more than 250 pots a week. In 2013 he was down to about 40, mostly due to a decrease in demand. Nicanor sells or barters his pots in the town of Jungay (205) some 20 km north from his home, and in Huaraz (206) the biggest town in the valley, in the Callejón de Huaylas, Ancash, Peru.

205

206

When well fired, a pot will 'ring' when struck with the finger. This 'ring' assures buyers there are no cracks or other defects.

207 Buying pots in the market of Beypazarı, Central Anatolia, Turkey.

208 Cooking pots for stew, rice, vegetable dish (round) and oval fish pan.

209 Portable cooking stoves, metal stoves with a ceramic plate on top, Beypazarı, Turkey.

Street Kitchens

Earthenware cooking pots are still used in daily life in many countries, at home, in restaurants and street kitchens. The photograph below was taken in the Grand Bazaar in Istanbul (210). Note the use of an electric plate to heat the stew in the ceramic pot while the aluminum pan is set on the gas stove. There is a prevalent belief that earthenware will not withstand a gas flame, which is not true. The same is observed in the Andes, out of social stigma. In the rural areas, earthenware pots are used on wood fires while aluminum pots are a sign of higher status, signifying that you have gas at home. There is a reverse trend in the cities, where it is fashionable to serve a local dish in an earthen pot. However, everyone agrees that a meal cooked in an earthenware pot tastes better, and especially on a woodstove.

210

211 A street kitchen in the San Pablo market, offering stew, soup and other traditional meals. Cajamarca Department, highland Peru.

212 Small food cart with cooking pots and individual stoves, Bangkok, Thailand.

213 Buffet at a big restaurant serving local food in Hanoi, Vietnam. The casseroles are kept warm by a flame inside the earthenware *brazeros*.

Special pots for special drinks

In China, the best teapots are made in Yixing, Jiangsu Province. Due to the quality of the clay and the porosity of the body that will preserve taste, connoisseurs reserve a teapot for a particular tea, and thus may own several for different teas. Ding Shu is the actual town within Yi Xin region, where most of the production takes place, with 70% of the 30.000 inhabitants involved in the trade. The purple sandy clay is famous for teapot production and comes from Huang Long Mountain 5 km from the center. Clay layers vary in color and firing temperature will bring out pots with yellow to reddish, brown and green tones. Xu Zhong Kun (below) and his wife Xu Jun Yin are specialists in teapot production. Their parents were also potters. At 16, they followed a three-year apprenticeship in a factory school, and continued learning with renowned master potters. In the old times, children would learn the trade already in middle school. The couple owns a small shop where they manufacture and sell their teapots. However, decoration is done by a specialist who learned the skill in a different school.

214

215

216 Teapots from Yi Xin and chocolate colored kneaded clay ball.

217   218

Fragment of one of the five clay types found in Huang Long Mountain (217) and the resulting clay color when fired (218).

219 Stand offering chicha beer in an earthenware jar in a fair in Lima, Peru.

Chicha, is another traditional drink that commands the use of different vessels, to ferment, transport, and serve it. Chicha is a common fermented drink present at all social events. It is an old custom, and brewing sites have been found in Peru dating to the Middle Horizon (AD 600-1100). It is made with sprouted corn but can also be made with *Shinus molle* seeds (Peruvian pepper tree - see Laffey 2015 or Justin and Bowser 2009 for more details).

220 A neighbor borrows a big jar to prepare chicha, the corn beer of the Andes. Ichikchinlla, Ancash, Peru.

221 Chicha fermenting in a jar, Huari, Ancash, Peru.

Traditionally, to brew and serve chicha, earthenware jars were used. This is still the case (219), but plastic jerricans are now also used for the fermenting stage in some places. If the practice generalizes, this could endanger the production of the chicha jars.

222 Earthenware miniature from Chulucanas, Piura, Peru. Woman serving chicha. Collection Bollinger, Lima, Peru.

223 Large jar to hold or transport liquid. The handles and the little protuberance like a nipple serve to hold a rope in place when transporting the jar on the back. Acopalca, Ancash, Peru.

224 Stoneware jars in the open kitchen at the back of a river boat, Guilin, China. A tasting bowl covers the lid and is typically used to taste the pickles to determine when they are mature. Water surrounding the bowl prevents air penetration. Ceramic, plastic, basket and aluminum pan are all part of kitchen inventory now.

225 Unsuccessful but still useful. This jar warped during firing but is used to support a pole in Phu Lang Vietnam, the village where it was produced. This type of jar usually stores pickled food or fish sauce. The presence of warped, cracked, overfired or underfired ceramics -and quantity of it, is an indication of a production site. Broken ceramics often serve other functions than the original one, such as storage containers, pails for animals or plants, or to protect walls or roof tops. Some are even crushed and recycled as temper for ceramic production.

226 Cooking pots and frying pans in a kitchen in the highlands of Cajamarca, Peru. The black is soot from carbon deposits and direct exposure to the flames when cooking.

Often a pot is reserved for a certain dish. Before the first use, it is usually necessary to cure it, with lime for example, to seal off the pores.

227 Cooking with earthenware, Acopalca, Ancash, Peru.

Further reading

Duncan, Ronald. 1998. *The ceramics of Ráquira, Colombia. Gender, work and economic change*. University Press of Florida. Gainsville.

Jennings, Justin and Brenda J. Bowser. 2009. *Drink, power and society in the Andes*. University of Florida Press, Gainesville, Fl.

Laffey, Ann. 2015. The residues of power: Women, chicha, and agency in the Middle Horizon Andes c. AD 600 – 1100. In *Ceramic Analysis in the Andes*, I. Druc (ed.), pp. 83-101. Deep University Press, WI.

Rooney, Dawne F. 1987. *Folk pottery in South-East Asia*. Oxford University Press, Oxford. (See in particular her comments on Yixing teapots and use of traditional pottery).

Video

Druc, Isabelle. 2010. *Special Turkish wares. Interview with Ayşegül Türedi Özen, ceramist*. https://vimeo.com/147800019.

228 Set of stoneware jars for collecting water (large mouth), liquid storage, pickling, transporting and serving. Viet Palace, Hanoi, Vietnam.

229 Wine jars, religious offerings, Tam Coc, Ninh Binh province, northern Vietnam.

9 A pot under a microscope

Ceramics are made of clay, but not all clays are equal and they often need to be modified, either by refining them or adding some other material to adjust for plasticity or workability. Furthermore, potters may choose to mix certain materials and not others and to prepare clay bodies following specific norms. It is the same for all the steps of production. These choices are embedded in and influenced by tradition, common practice, the technology used (hand building or wheel throwing for example) and the materials themselves. Looking at a ceramic paste under a microscope is one way to learn more about traditional manufacture. The resolution of regular microscopes does not permit one to easily view the clay: a material composed of about 80% clay minerals. plus other very fine material of different mineral species (Velde and Druc 1999). Clay minerals refer to a range of aluminium phyllosilicate minerals of minute size (c. 0.002 mm or less), which make up the montmorillonite, smectite, illite, kaolin and other clays. They are best studied with a scanning electron microscope. However, the larger inclusions, mineral or organic, can be observed with a simple microscope looking at a fresh cross section: a fragment you just broke from a pot so the surface is clean from any dirt that would mask the view. The grains, their size and distribution are then readily visible.

230 Digital portable low-power microscope connected to a computer where the image can be displayed and studied with image analysis softwares.

118 A pot under a microscope

More details can be obtained if we look at a ceramic paste with a petrographic microscope. For this, one needs to cut a small piece of the ceramic and have it prepared as a thin section. The ceramic fragment is consolidated in epoxy (an adhesive polymer), glued to a glass slide, thinned and polished to 30 microns (0.03mm). The light of the microscope shines through the thin section and the different minerals and grains in the paste can be observed. Each has specific characteristics, forms, and colors that enable the analyst to identify them. Archaeologists rely on this technique to study ancient ceramics and understand how they were manufactured. In addition, it highlights some of the choices the potters made. For example, it would show if they sieved and controlled the size of their material or if coils were used. One may also seek information regarding where the vessel may have been produced based upon the minerals and rock fragments it contains, which can often be linked to a certain region, type of sediment or rock formation. Thus the importance of knowing the local geology of an area. Sometimes, it is the voids left by plants like straw or rice husk after firing the pots that are the most interesting. They tell us not only about potting traditions - adding fibers as temper - but also of the concurrent activities taking place in the potters' community. The photographs presented here offer a glimpse into that world.

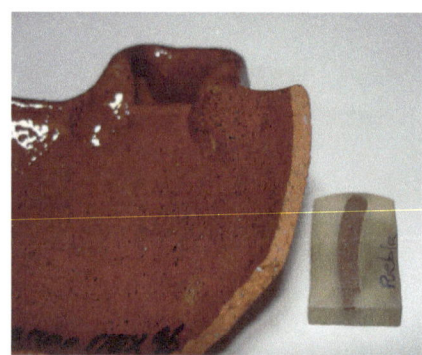

232

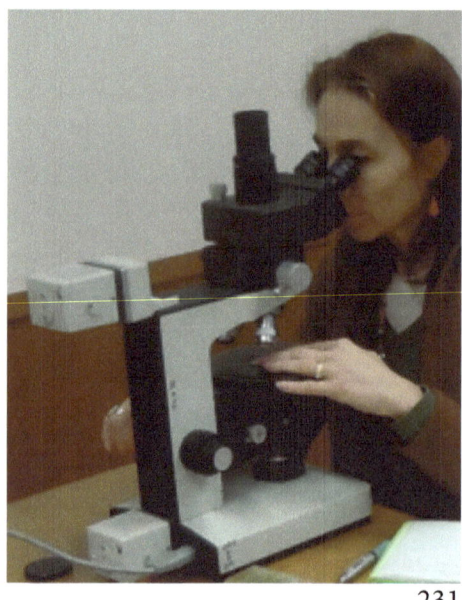

231

233

231 Petrographic microscope.

232 Stub of a ceramic fragment in a cast of epoxy resin.

233 Thin section mounted on a glass slide and cut ceramic fragment.

A pot under a microscope 119

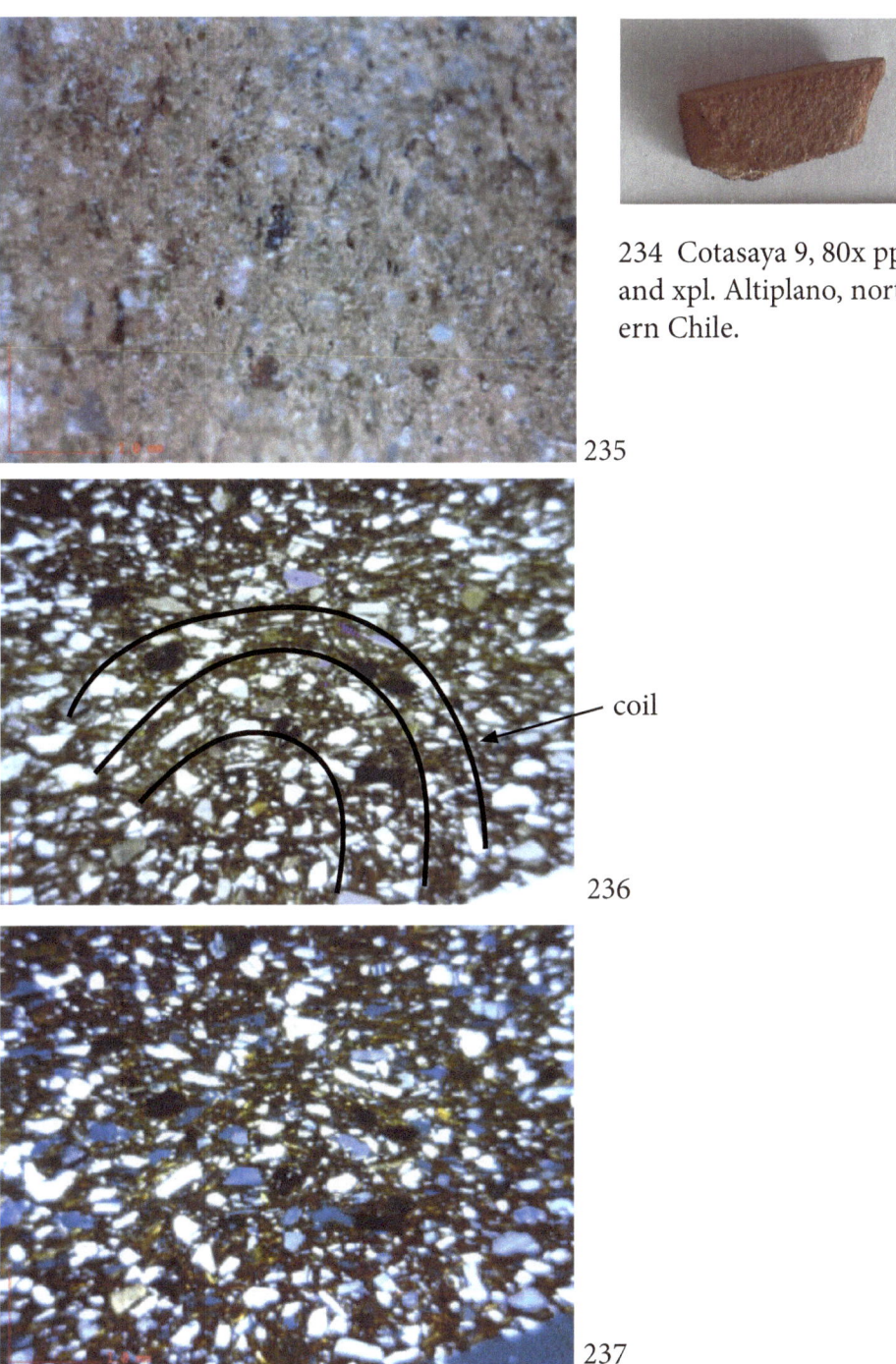

234 Cotasaya 9, 80x ppl and xpl. Altiplano, northern Chile.

235

236

237

235 Ceramic paste as seen with a low-power digital microscope (DinoLite) using reflective light (the light shines from above). The same sample can be studied with a petrographic microscope, more powerful and with the light shining from below (transmitted light). The sample can be observed in plain (236) or cross polarized light (237). The circular distribution of the grains in one part of the fragment suggests the use of the coiling technique to build the ware (black lines).

120 A pot under a microscope

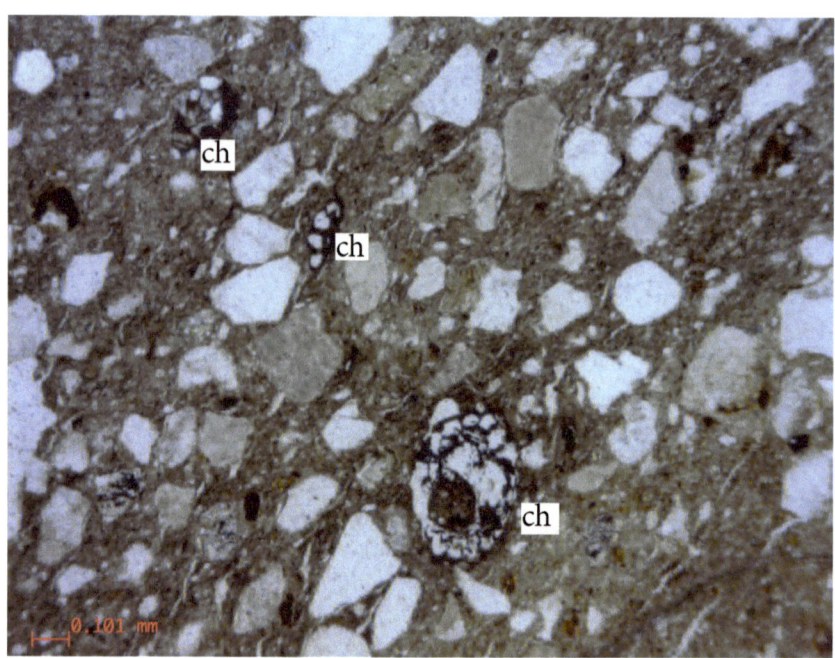
238

239   0 _____5cm

238 Ceramic paste of a 2500 year old bowl from Puemape (239), an archaeological site on the north coast of Peru. The three oval black and white grains in the center of the photograph are remains of an algae, a charophyte (ch), that grows in low-salty, calm waters. Their presence in the ceramic paste suggests that clay from a nearby lagoon must have been used to manufacture the vessel. Oxides (in black) delineate the form while the white areas enclosed are voids left from the burning out of the organic material upon firing. The largest charophyte seed is 0.35mm long. The other inclusions in the clay body are coastal sand grains. Transmitted light view, plain polarized light. PU177.

A pot under a microscope 121

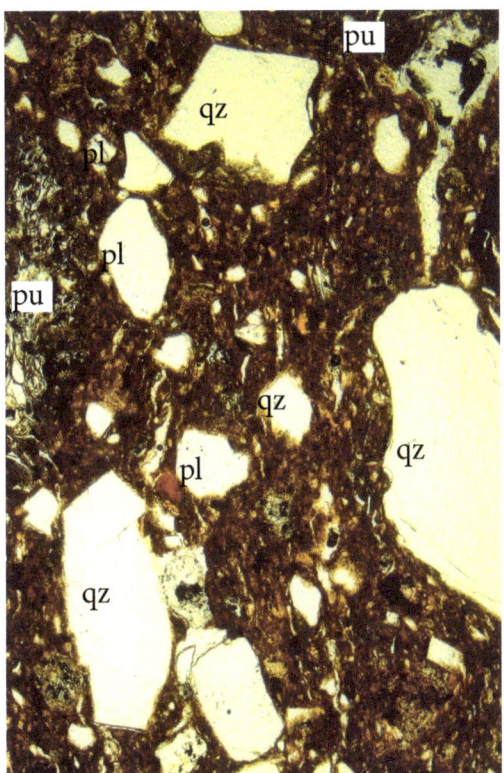
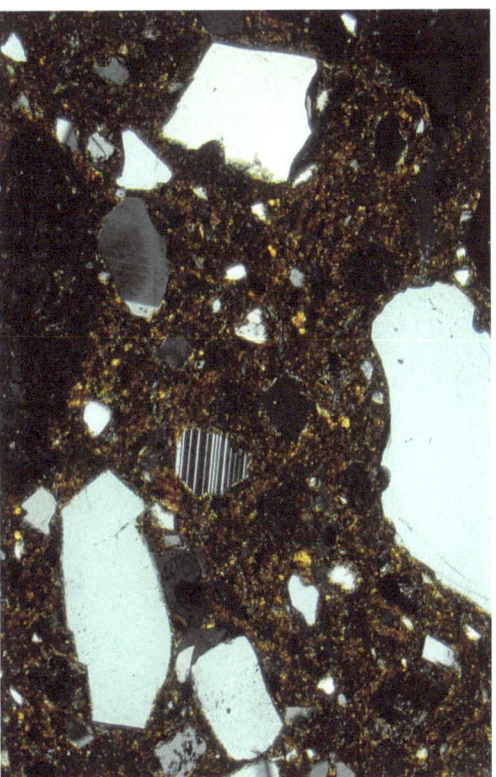

240-241 Thin section from a cooking pot from Mangallpa, Peru, tempered with volcanic material. Quartz (qz), plagioclase (pl), and pumice (pu) fragments in a micaceous clay matrix (brown background). Ma27 25x plain polarized light (240) and cross polarized light (241).

242 Potter Tanta Sánchez Mendoza with a stack of cooking pots tempered with the type of volcanic material as illustrated above. The black spots on the otherwise red ceramics are indication that the wares were exposed to direct flame when firing them. The red surface is also typical of an oxidizing firing, on the ground.

Further reading

Druc, Isabelle. 2015. *Portable digital microscope. Atlas of ceramic pastes. Components, texture and technology* (with the technical collaboration of B. Velde and L. Chavez). Deep University Press, Blue Mounds, WI.

Quinn, Patrick S. 2013. *Ceramic petrography. The interpretation of archaeological pottery and related artefacts in thin section.* Archaeopress, Oxford.

Velde, Bruce and Isabelle Druc. 1999. *Archaeological Ceramic Materials.* Springer Verlag, Berlin.

Video

Druc, Isabelle. 2009. *Ceramic petrography an interview with Dr. Jim Stoltman.* https://vimeo.com/search?q=ceramic+petrography.

243 Small workshop in Cuenca, Ecuador, using the kick wheel to turn the pots. The foot kicks the plate below and gives momentum to the wheel.

10 Conclusion

Traditional productions form a vital bridge between past and present. As ceramics still play an important role in many cultures, so do the persons who manufacture them. The different examples of potters and their work presented here show not only how diverse the conditions, organization, technology and types of ware produced are, but also how skillful, adaptive and hard working these craftspeople are. The more we learn about them and ceramic production, the more complex the picture. Ceramic making is not an isolated process. Production and distribution are embedded in the matrix of society itself, in the social relationships that shape trade partnership, producer-consumer links, work organization, which all can change with time and circumstances. What we eat and drink, the way food is prepared also affect the form and type of ceramics produced.

The status of potters may change from one culture to another, or one context to the next. In a majority of cases, the profession does not bring high status, nor large revenues. Many potters have difficult time making ends meet and have a low socio-economic status. There are exceptions however, notably in countries where ceramic making is considered a national art and ceramic masters are revered, like in China and Japan. These remarks are true for high end productions, less so for potters making domestic, utilitarian wares for the common people. As well, potters often live in the outskirts of cities and villages, or are clustered in communities manufacturing a whole range of utilitarian and/or decorative products or, on the contrary, specialized in producing one kind of ware. This peripheral location is in great part due to the space needed for production, material storage, drying areas, and to the firing and resulting smoke. In the past, potters producing for the elite, a ruler, or temple would typically have their workshop closer to their patron, while potters supplying lower status markets would live away from the center. Producing in large quantities also requires easy access to resources or their delivery, and ware distribution calls for access to convenient transportation networks. These are important economic factors that determine the location of a production center. Isolated or village potters producing for their community operate at a different scale, in terms of intensity, resource procurement, and standardization. There, the logic of production does not always correspond to our

124 Conclusion

logic of productivity. The resources used might not be the closest available, nor the best, faster ways of producing are not necessarily selected and activities or work schedule may follow a ritual or socio-cultural timeframe.

Finally, looking at traditional craft production offers a way to envision ancient productions when no written records exist. It gives a face to those who produced the thousands of ceramic vessels and objects that we still admire today, utilitarian, ceremonial, in burials, for the commoner and the elite. *Mingei*, the art of the people, evolves with us. It will endure as long as we respect singularity, localism, non-global practices, and favor small scale worshops over faceless industries.

Acknowledgements

I am indebted to all the persons who made these studies and travels possible. The potters, of course, but also my family, colleagues, funding agencies, friends, and guides who accompanied me and, when needed, helped translate my questions and the replies. Every time possible, the potters interviewed were revisited, given photographs, articles, videos or the book which included some of the information they gave me. Thus, with deep acknowledgement of their skills, I wish to thank the potters, as well as the colleagues and friends who taught me much more than how a pot is formed. I also want to acknowledge Janine Kam for her revision as well as ceramist Andrée Valley for her insightful remarks when reading the manuscript, and for our discussions about firing and ceramic technology.

DEEP UNIVERSITY PRESS SCIENTIFIC BOARD MEMBERS

Dr. Araceli Alonso, Global Health Institute, Department of Gender and Women's Studies, University of Wisconsin-Madison, USA
Dr. Ronald C. Arnett, Chair and Professor, Department of Communication & Rhetorical Studies, Duquesne University
Dr. Gilles Baillat, Rector, ex-Director of CDIUFM Conference of French Teacher Education Directors, University of Reims, France
Dr. Niels Brouwer, Graduate School of Education, Radboud Universiteit Nijmegen, The Netherlands
Dr. Jianlin Chen, Shanghai International Studies University, China
Dr. Yuangshan Chuang, President of APAMALL, NETPAW Director, Tajen University, Taiwan, ROC
Dr. Enrique Correa Molina, Professor and Vice-Dean, Faculty of Education, University of Sherbrooke, Canada
Dr. José Correia, Dean of Education, University of Porto, Portugal
Dr. Muhammet Demirbilek, Head, Educational Science Department, Suleyman Demirel University, Isparta, Turkey
Dr. Ángel Díaz-Barriga Casales, Professor, Autonomous National University of México UNAM (Mexico)
Dr. Isabelle C. Druc, Department of Anthropology, University of Wisconsin-Madison, USA
Bertha Du-Babcock, Professor, Department of English for Business, City University of Hong Kong, Hong Kong, China
Dr. W. John Coletta, Professor, University of Wisconsin-Stevens Point, USA
Marc Durand, Professor, Faculty of Psychology and Education, University of Geneva, Switzerland
Dr. Paul Durning, Doctoral School, French National Observatory, EUSARF, University of Paris X Nanterre, Paris, France
Dr. Manuel Fernandez Cruz, Professor, University of Granada, Spain
Dr. Stephanie Fonvielle, Associate Professor, Teacher Education University Institute, University of Aix-Marseille, France
Dr. Elliot Gaines, Professor, Wright State University, President of the Semiotic Society of America, Internat. Communicology Institute
Dr. Mingle Gao, Dean, College of Education, Beijing Language and Culture University (BLCU), Beijing, China
Dr. Mercedes González Sanmamed, Professor at the University of Coruña, Spain
Dr. Gabriela Hernández Vega, Professor, University of Nariño, Colombia.

Dr. Teresa Langle de Paz, Autonomous University, Feminist Research Institute Council, Complutense University of Madrid, Spain
Dr. Xiang Long, Guilin University of Electronic Technology, China
Dr. Maria Masucci, Drew University, New Jersey, USA
Dr. Liliana Morandi, Associate Professor, National University of Rio Cuarto, Cordoba, Argentina
Dr. Joëlle Morrissette, Professor, Department of Educational Psychology, Université of Montreal, Quebec, Canada
Dr. Martha Murzi Vivas, Professor, University of Los Andes, Venezuela
Dr. Thi Cuc Phuong Nguyen, Vice Rector, Hanoi University, Vietnam
Dr. Shirley O'Neill, Associate Professor, President of the International Society for leadership in Pedagogies and Learning, University of Southern Queensland, Australia
Dr. José-Luis Ortega, Professor, Foreign Language Education, Faculty of Education, University of Granada, Spain
Dr. Surendra Pathak, Head and Professor, Department of Value Education, IASE University of Gandhi Viday Mandir, India
Dr. Charls Pearson, Logic, Semiotics, Philosophy of Science, Peirce Studies, Director of Research, Semiotics Research Institute
Dr. Luis Porta Vázquez, Professor at the National University of Mar del Plata CONICET (Argentina)
Dr. Shen Qi, Associate Professor, Shanghai Foreign Studies University (SHISU), Shanghai, China
Dr. Timothy Reagan, Professor and Dean of the College of Education at Zayed University in Abu Dhabi/Dubai, Saudi Arabia
Dr. Farouk Y. Seif, Exec. Director of the Semiotic Society of America, Center for Creative Change, Antioch University Seattle, Washington
Dr. Gary Shank, Professor, Educational Foundations and Leadership, Duquesne University, Pittsburgh, Pennsylvania
Dr. Kemal Silay, Professor, Flagship Program Director, Department of Central Eurasia, Indiana University-Bloomington, USA
Dr. José Tejada Fernández, Professor at the Autonomous University of Barcelona, Spain
Dr. Jianfang Xiao, Associate Professor at School of English and Education, Guangdong University of Foreign Studies, China.
Dr. Ronghui Zhao, Director, Institute of Linguistic Studies, Shanghai Foreign Studies University, Shanghai, China
Other referees may be contacted depending the Book Series or the nature and topic of the manuscript proposed.

AT DEEP UNIVERSITY PRESS

Portable Digital Microscope
ATLAS OF CERAMIC PASTES
COMPONENTS, TEXTURE AND TECHNOLOGY

Isabelle C. Druc

with the technical collaboration of
Bruce Velde and Lisenia Chavez

This manual is the first of its sort describing the use of the new portable digital microscope for analysis of archaeological ceramics in the field or in the laboratory. It is presented like a geological atlas with a description of the most common minerals and lithic fragments found in ancient ceramic pastes to help archaeologists identify what they see under the microscope. Identification of manufacture and technological features are also addressed. An analytic protocol is proposed along with further suggestions for granulometric and digital image analyses to help with the constitution of groups of similar composition and paste texture. The manual is abundantly illustrated with pictures of archaeological and ethnographic ceramic pastes and raw materials. It is a reference book for all involved in the analysis of archaeological ceramics and a major tool to help study, classify and choose the best fragments for archaeometric analysis.

"This timely and valuable contribution led by Dr Isabelle Druc, a renowned ceramic specialist, brings the spotlight back to the study of pottery and its myriad relationships with people. This handy guide will be useful for both students and professionals interested in learning to investigate, with precision, the composition of raw materials and their transformation by people. It enables the identification and description of their choices that inform about the critical stuff (techniques, identity, values, landscape) of ancient cultures. "

George Lau, Sainsbury Research Unit, University of East Anglia, UK

"Given the increased accessibility of tools such as portable microscopes, this book provides timely and very useful guidelines for macroscopic analysis of ceramic paste. With its detailed illustrations, descriptions of diagnostic features for different kinds of minerals, and holistic approach to systems of ceramic production, I believe the book will be regarded as essential to consult for initial research on paste composition in many areas."

Anne Underhill, Yale University

ISBN 978-1-939755-07-0
(Paperback)

Edited volume

CERAMIC ANALYSIS IN THE ANDES

Isabelle C. Druc (ed)

The panorama and diversity of research presented in this volume testify to the vitality of ceramic analysis in Andean archaeology. It highlights the work of leading scholars and younger archaeologists conducting investigations mostly in Peru and Chile, combining a variety of mineral and chemical studies to investigate socio-political and cultural questions, issues of political control, intra- and intervalley interactions, and expressions of cultural traditions and social identities in the ancient Andes.

The different chapters cover a large time frame, from the 1st millennium BC to the Inca period, while ethnographic and experimental studies supply additional invaluable information for the interpretation of the archaeological data. As well, this volume offers an overview of the sampling strategies and analytical techniques currently used in Andean studies for material analysis, of the diversity of paste types and geoenvironments observed for the regions studied, and of the expected mineral and chemical compositions in the study areas.

With chapters by Mauricio Uribe Rodríguez and Estefanía Vidal Montero; Isabelle Druc; Michele L. Koons; Ann O. Laffey; Matthew Piscitelli, Sofia Chacaltana Cortez, Nicola Sharratt, Mark Golitko, and Patrick Ryan Williams; Jason L. Toohey; Krzysztof Makowski, Ivan Ghezzi, Hector Neff, and Gabriela Ore; and Mary F. Ownby.

ISBN 978-1-939755-11-7, 7.44 x 9.69 in (189 x 246 mm), 190 pages, 85 color figures, maps and diagrams, 10 chapters.

Deep University Press http://www.deepuniversitypress.org/ceramic.html

Deep University Press Books

Out of Havana: Memoirs of Ordinary Life in Cuba

Dr. Araceli Alonso
University of Wisconsin-Madison

Out of Havana provides an uncommon ordinary woman's insight into the last half century of Cuba's tumultuous recent history. More powerfully than an academic study or historical account, it allows us intimately to grasp the enthusiasm, commitment and sense of promise that defined many average Cubans' experience of the 1959 Revolution and the first triumphant decades of the Castro regime. As the story shifts into the final decades of the last century (the 1980s Mariel Boatlift, the so-called "special period in time of peace" [from 1991 to the end of the decade], and the 1994 Balseros or Rafters Crisis), it starts gradually to reveal, with understated yet relentless eloquence, an ultimately insuperable rift between the high-flown official rhetoric of uncompromising struggle and revolutionary sacrifice and the harsh conditions and cruelly absurd situations that the protagonist, along with the majority of Cubans, begin routinely to live out. It is a rare and important document, a unique personal chronicle of an everyday Cuban reality that most Americans continue to know only fragmentarily.

Dr. Araceli Alonso is a 2013 United Nations Award Winner for her activism on women's health and women right. Associate Faculty at the University of Wisconsin-Madison in the Department of Gender and Women's Studies and in the School of Medicine and Public Health, she is the Founder and Director of the award-winning non-profit organization Health by Motorbike.

http://deepuniversitypress.org/havana.html

Science Teachers Who Draw: The Red Is Always There

Dr. Merrie Koester
Project Draw for Science
Center for Science Education
University of South Carolina

This book documents the ways in which science teacher researchers used drawing to construct semiotic spaces inside which students acquired significant aesthetic capital and agency. Many previously failing students brokered this new capital into improved academic achievement and a sense of felt freedom.

Science Teachers Who Draw: The Red is Always There is a book which asks, "What happens when science teachers adopt an aesthetic approach to inquiry, using drawing to communicate deep understanding?" This narrative inquiry was driven by quantitative studies which reveal a robust positive correlation between students' test scores in reading and science, beginning at the middle school level. When the data are disaggregated, there exists a vast achievement gap for low income and English language learners. Science teachers are faced with a semiotic nightmare. Often possessing inadequate pedagogical content knowledge themselves, science teachers must somehow symbolically communicate often highly abstract knowledge in ways that can be not only be decoded by their students' but later used to construct deeper, more differentiated knowledge, which can be applied to make sense of and adapt successfully to life on Planet Earth.

An invaluable resource for teachers, teacher educators,
and qualitative researchers.

http://www.deepuniversity.net/koester.html
http://www.deepuniversitypress.org/red.html

TRANSFER OF LEARNING AND THE CULTURAL MATRIX
Culture, Beliefs and Learning in Thailand Higher Education

Dr. Jonathan H. Green
University of Southern Queensland

The field of quality teaching and learning is a complex and dynamic one. Jonathan Green's book on the transfer of learning makes an original contribution to this field in that it adds value to the discourse on influences and forces impacting on quality student learning. Learning is not a one-directed process, characterised by teacher-centeredness, but one where students are at the centre. Understanding how students perceive and experience their own learning is a key to unlocking their potential. This is a long-overdue publication.

Professor Arend E. Carl, Vice-Dean: Teaching, Stellenbosch University, South Africa

Through this research, Jonathan Green has contributed to the body of knowledge about transfer of learning. His rigorous research investigates transfer in the context of learners' personal epistemology and culture, yielding a culturally relative understanding of transfer that is highly relevant in today's increasingly diverse classrooms. The findings, which have implications for educators in a wide range of educational contexts, will be of particular interest to those who teach in internationalized and multicultural institutions.

Alexander Nanni, Director, Preparation Center for Languages and Mathematics at Mahidol University International College, Thailand

Original thought provoking, high quality research that extends our knowledge of transfer of learning in relation to multicultural tertiary students in international education settings. Deep insights are gained, through use of the researcher's Measure of Academic Literacy (MALT), a new tool that explored issues of context and cultural values and beliefs, and metacognitive knowledge in transfer of learning.

Associate Professor Shirley O'Neill, Applied Linguistics Discipline Coordinator, School of Linguistics, Adult and Specialist Education, University of Southern Queensland

http://www.deepuniversitypress.org/transfer.html

SIGNS AND SYMBOLS IN EDUCATION
François Victor Tochon, Ph.D.
University of Wisconsin-Madison, USA

In this monograph on Educational Semiotics, François Tochon (along with a number of research colleagues) has produced a work that is truly groundbreaking on a number of fronts. First of all, in his concise but brilliant introductory comments, Tochon clearly debunks the potential notion that semiotics might provide yet another methodological tool in the toolkit of educational researchers. Drawing skillfully on the work of Peirce, Deely, Sebeok, Merrell, and others, Tochon shows us just how fundamentally different semiotic research can be when compared to the modes and techniques that have dominated educational research for many decades. That is, he points out how semiotic methods can provide the capability for both students and researchers to look at this basic and fundamental human process in inescapably transformational ways, by acknowledging and accepting that the path to knowledge is, in his words "through the fixation of belief."

But he does not stop there – instead, in four brilliantly conceived studies, he shows us how semiotic concepts in general, and semiotic mapping in particular, can allow both student teachers and researchers alike insights in these students' development of insights and concepts into the very heart of the teaching and learning process. By tackling both theoretical and practical research considerations, Tochon has provided the rest of us the beginnings of a blueprint that, if adopted, can push educational research out of (in the words of Deely) its entrenchment in the Age of Ideas into the new and exciting frontiers of the Age of Signs.

Gary Shank, Duquesne University

See reviews here:

FROM TRANSNATIONAL LANGUAGE POLICY TRANSFER TO LOCAL APPROPRIATION

The case of the National Bilingual Program in Medellín, Colombia

Dr. Jaime Usma Wilches

University of Antioquia

Embracing a critical and sociocultural perspective for the study of policy, this vertical case study investigates foreign language education policies being adopted by the national government in Colombia, and how they are reinterpreted and appropriated by local official and public school teachers in the city of Medellín.
ISBN 978-1-939755-20-9 (hb)

Maria Alfredo Moreira, University of Minho, Portugal:
Drawing on the example of Medellín, Colombia, Jaime Usma's book does a magnificent work at dismantling one of the most pervasive grand narratives in globalized transnational foreign language policies: proficiency in English as one of the strongest pillars of a vibrant modern knowledge society, associated with higher economic gains for all. The author cogently demonstrates how apparently neutral and technically sound transnational and national policymaking fails to properly address structural inequality and social and economic injustice, while being creatively reenacted by local schools and actors that appropriate them according to their own goals, needs, and desires towards a more just and humane society.

Doris Correa, Associate Professor, Universidad de Antioquia, Medellin, Colombia:
Usma's book is much more than a nice rendition of how transnational language policies are being appropriated by government officials and other educational actors in Colombia. It is an enjoyable journey into Colombia's most recent political, socio-economic and educational reforms, and a compelling critical analysis of how those reforms are influencing school and classroom practices in Medellin.

Anikó Hatoss, University of New South Wales, Sydney, Australia:
This volume represents much needed scholarship in exploring the tensions between official language policies and their practical implementation on the ground. While these tensions have long been the interest of language policy studies, it is rare that scholars explore them through such rigorous and multilayered empirical research capturing the global and local. The comparative and critical lens applied here makes this volume an outstanding contribution to the field and provides invaluable insights for researchers, policy makers, curriculum planners and language teaching practitioners about language education in Columbia with lessons to be learnt far beyond.

Archaeological Depth and Anthropology Book Series

This book series is oriented toward publishing full-length, peer-reviewed investigations in archaeology and anthropology, including ethnoarchaeological and ethnographic studies. It offers a platform for sharing analytical approaches and the results of in-depth multidisciplinary material studies integrated to larger research questions with the aim of better understanding ancient society at large. A holistic approach, however, goes beyond the object to recognize the artisan. Craft people form communities of practices with technological traditions operating within particular socio-cultural, economic and ideological settings. Highlighting their work by way of detailed mineral and chemical analysis is one way to apprehend and give credit to the human dimension behind materiality.

Authors wishing to publish in English, Spanish, French or German are welcome.

For more, see: http://deepuniversity.com/archaeologicaldepth.html

Book Series on Deep Research Methodologies

Research methodologies need to be reconceptualized in two ways: first, as the expression of dynamic interpretive prototypes that can be activated through deep forms of inquiry that go beyond the surface level at which meanings are essentialized and reified. Second, integrating emergent technologies, structure and agency to meet deeper, humane aims. The dynamism of human interpretation is meaning-producing through multiple connected intentions among disciplinary domains.

By tackling both theoretical and practical research considerations, this book series provides the readers a blueprint that can push research into the new and exciting frontiers of the Age of Signs (in the words of Gary Shank). Taking into account adaptive and complex situations is the prime focus of such a hermeneutic inquiry.

The intent of this book series is to propose instruments to analyze beyond the surface of the matter in favor of value-loaded investigations chosen in order to revolutionize the current state of affairs, in increasing our sense of responsibility for our actions as humans vis-à-vis our fellow humans and our home planet.

For more see:
http://www.deepuniversitypress.org/deep-research-methodologies.html

Deep University Online !

For updates and more resources
Visit the Deep University Website:

www.deepuniversity.net
www.deepunversitypress.org
Contact: publisher@deepuniversity.net

Online Certificate and Courses on Deep Education:
http://www.deepuniversity.net/graduatecourses.html

Correspondence for this volume:
Isabelle C. Druc, Department of Anthropology, 5240 Social Science,
1180 Observatory Dr., University of Wisconsin-Madison,
Madison, Wisconsin 53706 USA.
E-mail: icdruc@wisc.edu

Guide to Authors

What our Publishing Team can offer:

- An international editorial team, in more than 20 universities around the world.
- Dedicated and experienced topic editors who will review and provide feedback on your initial proposal.
- A specific format that will speed up the production of your book and its publication.
- Higher royalties than most publishers and a discount on batch orders.
- Global distribution and marketing in the U.S., UK, Europe, Australia, Brazil, China, Japan, South Korea and other countries.
- Fast recognition of your work in your area of specialization.
- Quality design and affordable sales pricing. Using the latest technology, our books are produced efficiently, quickly and attractively.
- A global marketing plan, including electronic and web marketing and review mailing.
- Book Series: Deep Education; Deep Language Learning; Signs & Symbols in Education; Language Education Policy; Deep Professional Development; Deep Activism, Archaeological Depth and Anthropology.
- http://www.deepuniversitypress.org/guide.html
- Contact : publisher@deepuniversity.net

Isabelle C. Druc did her Ph.D. in Archaeology at the University of Montreal (Quebec, Canada), after finishing her initial studies in Switzerland. She is specialized in ceramic studies, Andean archaeology, and ethnoarchaeological research. She did her post-doctoral studies at Yale University in the United States, and has been a visiting scholar at the CNRS in France and at the Smithsonian in Washington D.C. She has received two excellence awards from the University of Montreal in Canada and won the 1989 Plantamour-Prévost science prize in Switzerland for her master at the University of Geneva. She has been at the University of Wisconsin-Madison since 2000, holding positions of lecturer and honorary fellow in the Department of Anthropology, and associate researcher in the Wisconsin Center for Education Research (WCER). She has been involved in many archaeological projects and ethnographic studies in South America, the USA, Europe, the Middle East, China and Southeast Asia, has published thirty articles and eight books as author, co-author, or editor, and has produced some 200 film documentaries and video interviews related to culture, ceramics, traditional arts, handicrafts, and language.

www.ingramcontent.com/pod-product-compliance
Lightning Source LLC
Chambersburg PA
CBHW041152290426

44108CB00002B/42